First World War
and Army of Occupation
War Diary
France, Belgium and Germany

20 DIVISION
Divisional Troops
83 Field Company Royal Engineers
22 July 1915 - 31 May 1919

WO95/2107/1

The Naval & Military Press Ltd
www.nmarchive.com
Published in association with The National Archives

Published by

The Naval & Military Press Ltd

Unit 10 Ridgewood Industrial Park,

Uckfield, East Sussex,

TN22 5QE England

Tel: +44 (0) 1825 749494

www.naval-military-press.com

www.nmarchive.com

This diary has been reprinted in facsimile from the original. Any imperfections are inevitably reproduced and the quality may fall short of modern type and cartographic standards.

© **Crown Copyright**
Images reproduced by permission of The National Archives, London, England, 2015.

Contents

Document type	Place/Title	Date From	Date To
Miscellaneous	2107/1		
Heading	20th Division Divl Engineers 83rd Field Coy R.E. Jly 1915-May 1919		
Heading	20th Division 83rd F.C.R.E. Vol. I July 22-30 July 15 May 19		
War Diary	Larkhill Smthangton	22/07/1915	24/07/1915
War Diary	Le Havre	25/07/1915	25/07/1915
War Diary	St Omer	26/07/1915	26/07/1915
War Diary	Boisdinghem	27/07/1915	28/07/1915
War Diary	Pradelles	29/07/1915	29/07/1915
War Diary	Oultersteene	30/07/1915	30/07/1915
Heading	20th Division 83rd F.C.R.E. Vol. II August 15		
War Diary	Oultersteene	31/07/1915	31/07/1915
War Diary	Merris	01/08/1915	09/08/1915
War Diary	Bac St Maur	10/08/1915	17/08/1915
War Diary	Rue De La Lys	18/08/1915	26/08/1915
War Diary	Laventie	27/08/1915	31/08/1915
Heading	20th Division 83rd F.C.R.E. Vol. III Sept 15		
War Diary	Laventie	01/09/1915	24/09/1915
War Diary	Near Chapigny Farm	25/09/1915	25/09/1915
War Diary	Laventie	26/09/1915	30/09/1915
Operation(al) Order(s)	Operation Order No. 7 By Major Le Hophin RE C/o 83 Neld Co		
Miscellaneous	Operation For 2nd		
Heading	20th Division 83rd F.C.R.E. Vol. 4 Oct 15		
War Diary	Laventie	01/10/1915	31/10/1915
Heading	20th Division 83rd F.C.R.E. Dec 15 Vol 5		
War Diary	Laventie	01/11/1915	20/11/1915
War Diary	Bac St Maur	21/11/1915	30/11/1915
Heading	20th Div. 83rd F.C.R.E. Vol 6		
War Diary	Bac St Maur	01/12/1915	31/12/1915
Heading	83rd F.C.R.E. Vol. 7		
War Diary	Bac St Maur	01/01/1916	11/01/1916
War Diary	Steen Becque	12/01/1916	22/01/1916
War Diary	Billets At P 24 A 7.4	23/01/1916	31/01/1916
War Diary	St Sylvestre Cappel	01/02/1916	05/02/1916
War Diary	Watou	06/02/1916	10/02/1916
War Diary	Elverdinghe	11/02/1916	29/02/1916
Diagram etc	Boesinghe		
Heading	83 F C R E Vol 9		
War Diary	Elverdinghe	01/03/1916	25/04/1916
War Diary	Winnezeele	26/04/1916	26/04/1916
War Diary	Calais	27/04/1916	30/04/1916
Miscellaneous	83rd F.C Coy. R.E	24/04/1916	24/04/1916
Miscellaneous	C Form (Duplicate) Messages And Signals		
Miscellaneous	O.C. 83rd Fd Coy RE	28/04/1916	28/04/1916
Miscellaneous	83rd Field Coy. R.E	24/04/1916	24/04/1916
Miscellaneous	83rd Fd Coy. R.E	23/04/1916	23/04/1916
Miscellaneous	To O.C. 83rd Field Coy R.E	25/04/1916	25/04/1916
Miscellaneous	O.C. 83rd Field Coy. R.E	21/04/1916	21/04/1916

Type	Description	Start	End
Operation(al) Order(s)	20th Divn Operation Order No. 54	19/04/1916	19/04/1916
War Diary	Calais	01/05/1916	09/05/1916
War Diary	Ledringhem	10/05/1916	15/05/1916
War Diary	Winnezeele	16/05/1916	18/05/1916
War Diary	Vlamertinghe	19/05/1916	19/05/1916
War Diary	Ypres	20/05/1916	31/05/1916
Heading	D.A.G. 3rd Echelon. Herewith War Diary of 83rd Field Co Re for the Period 1st to 30th June 1916		
War Diary	Ypres	01/06/1916	30/06/1916
Heading	20th Divisional Engineers 83rd Field Company R.E July 1916		
War Diary	Ypres	01/07/1916	15/07/1916
War Diary	Vlamertinghe	16/07/1916	16/07/1916
War Diary	Houtkerque	17/07/1916	18/07/1916
War Diary	Berthen	19/07/1916	19/07/1916
War Diary	Neuve Eglise	20/07/1916	20/07/1916
War Diary	Dranoutre	21/07/1916	21/07/1916
War Diary	St Jan Cappel	22/07/1916	30/07/1916
Heading	20th Divisional Engineers.83rd Field Company R.E. August 1916		
War Diary	Courcelles	31/07/1916	16/08/1916
War Diary	Amplier	16/08/1916	17/08/1916
War Diary	St. Hilaire	18/08/1916	20/08/1916
War Diary	Ville Sur Ancre	20/08/1916	21/08/1916
War Diary	Meaulte	22/08/1916	22/08/1916
War Diary	Carnoy	22/08/1916	30/08/1916
Heading	20th Divisional Engineers. 83rd Field Company R.E. September 1916		
War Diary	Carnoy	31/08/1916	06/09/1916
War Diary	Bray	07/09/1916	08/09/1916
War Diary	Vaux Sur Somme	09/09/1916	09/09/1916
War Diary	S. 23 C 5.3 Bernafay Wood Guillemont T. 92 2.3	17/09/1916	17/09/1916
War Diary	Guillemont	18/09/1916	18/09/1916
War Diary	Bernafay Wood	19/09/1916	19/09/1916
War Diary	Citadelle F.21. 9.5	20/09/1916	21/09/1916
War Diary	Vaux Sur Somme	10/09/1916	11/09/1916
War Diary	Meaulte	12/09/1916	14/09/1916
War Diary	F 21 A 5.7 (atached)	15/09/1916	15/09/1916
War Diary	Bois De Talus	15/09/1916	15/09/1916
War Diary	Bernafay Wood	16/09/1915	16/09/1915
War Diary	Reference Maps Albert F 21 A 8.4	22/09/1916	22/09/1916
War Diary	Treux	23/09/1916	25/09/1916
War Diary	F 21 A 8.4	26/09/1916	26/09/1916
War Diary	S 30 C 0.7 Trones Wood	27/09/1916	27/09/1916
War Diary	S 30 C O.7	28/09/1916	29/09/1916
War Diary	Longueval	30/09/1916	30/09/1916
Heading	20th Divisional Engineers. 83rd Field Company R.E October 1916		
Heading	83rd Field Coy Vol 16		
War Diary	Longueval	01/10/1916	09/10/1916
War Diary	Sand Pits F.19 Central	10/10/1916	15/10/1916
War Diary	Daours	16/10/1916	18/10/1916
War Diary	Citadel F21a	19/10/1916	19/10/1916
War Diary	Craters A 8a	20/10/1916	29/10/1916
Heading	20th Divisional Engineers 83rd Field Company R.E. November 1916		

War Diary	Craters (A8A)	30/10/1916	14/11/1916
War Diary	Corbie	15/11/1916	29/11/1916
Heading	20th Divisional Engineers 83rd Field Company R.E. December 1916		
War Diary	Corbie	30/11/1916	09/12/1916
War Diary	Treux	10/12/1916	10/12/1916
War Diary	Trones Wood	11/12/1916	30/12/1916
Heading	War Diary of The 83rd Field Company RE January 1917		
War Diary	Craters	31/12/1916	01/01/1917
War Diary	Bronfay Fm	01/01/1917	03/01/1917
War Diary	Wedge Wood	03/01/1917	27/01/1917
War Diary	Meaulte	28/01/1917	28/01/1917
War Diary	Heilly	29/01/1917	07/03/1917
War Diary	S 30. A	08/02/1917	29/04/1917
War Diary	Metz-En-Couture	01/05/1917	04/05/1917
War Diary	Dessart Wood W.1.b.2.4	13/05/1917	25/05/1917
War Diary	H 16 B 5.4	25/05/1917	27/05/1917
War Diary	C.20.a.0.0 Vraucourt	30/05/1917	29/06/1917
War Diary	Achiet-Le-Petit	30/06/1917	30/06/1917
War Diary	Camaples	01/07/1917	01/07/1917
War Diary	Camaples and Halloy-Les-Pernois	02/07/1917	08/07/1917
War Diary	Tirancourt	09/07/1917	12/07/1917
War Diary	Halloy-Les-Pernois	13/07/1917	20/07/1917
War Diary	E 17. D 6.4	21/07/1917	30/07/1917
War Diary	Boesinghe	31/07/1917	31/08/1917
War Diary	White Hope Corner	01/09/1917	07/09/1917
War Diary	Canal Bank Near Causeway	10/09/1917	29/09/1917
War Diary	Salem Camp	30/09/1917	29/11/1917
War Diary	Villers Plouich Map Lens II	30/11/1917	01/12/1917
War Diary	Sorel	02/12/1917	03/12/1917
War Diary	Varennes	04/12/1917	06/12/1917
War Diary	Gournay	07/12/1917	07/12/1917
War Diary	Map Hazebrouck 5a	09/12/1917	13/12/1917
War Diary	Le Crocquet	14/12/1917	16/12/1917
War Diary	Re. Farm Near Kemmel	17/12/1917	05/01/1918
War Diary	Jackdaw Tunnels J 19 A 8.9	06/01/1918	27/01/1918
War Diary	Jackdaw Tunnels	27/01/1918	30/01/1918
War Diary	Kroisstratt Near Dickebusch Sheet Hazebrouck 5A	31/01/1918	15/02/1918
War Diary	Racquinghem (Hazebrouck 5a)	16/02/1918	21/02/1918
War Diary	Ercheu Sheet Amiens	22/02/1918	27/02/1918
Heading	20th Divisional Engineers 83rd Field Company R.E. March 1918		
War Diary	Ercheu	01/03/1918	02/03/1918
War Diary	Sommette	03/03/1918	03/03/1918
War Diary	Eaucourt	04/03/1918	21/03/1918
War Diary	St. Sulpice	22/03/1918	23/03/1918
War Diary	Bacancourt	24/03/1918	24/03/1918
War Diary	Rethonvillers	25/03/1918	26/03/1918
War Diary	Hangest En-Santerre	27/03/1918	27/03/1918
War Diary	Domart-Sur-Luce	28/03/1918	29/03/1918
War Diary	Boves	30/03/1918	31/03/1918
Miscellaneous	O.C. 83rd Fld Coy R.E	06/04/1918	06/04/1918
Diagram etc	Sketch of Brigade Over River & Canat At Offoy		
War Diary	Boves Sheet Amiens	31/03/1918	12/04/1918
War Diary	Beauchamps	13/04/1918	17/04/1918

War Diary	Sheet Abbeville	18/04/1918	20/04/1918
War Diary	Gauchin-Le-Gal Sheet Lens ll	21/04/1918	29/04/1918
Miscellaneous	Infantry Programme 3 week ending 5th May		
Miscellaneous	Infantry Programme 2nd Lock		
War Diary	Gauchin Legal	01/05/1918	01/05/1918
War Diary	Carency-Souchez Rd X 17 B 4.2	02/05/1918	30/06/1918
War Diary	Malon Camp Carency-Souchez Rd X 17 B 4.2	01/07/1918	23/07/1918
War Diary	Malon Camp	22/07/1918	31/07/1918
War Diary	La Folie Wood S 2 C. 4.4	01/08/1918	24/08/1918
War Diary	Malon Camp Near Souchez X 17 B 4.2	01/09/1918	27/09/1918
Heading	1st Div 1st Bde Units October 1918		
War Diary	La Folie Wood S 23 C 44	01/10/1918	05/10/1918
War Diary	Estree Cauchie	06/10/1918	29/10/1918
War Diary	Cambrai	30/10/1918	31/10/1918
War Diary	Famechon (lens II 5f. 65. 72)	02/12/1918	31/12/1918
War Diary	Famechon	01/01/1919	31/01/1919
War Diary	Famechon Lens II (5 F.65.72)	01/02/1919	31/05/1919

2/07/11

**20TH DIVISION
DIVL ENGINEERS**

~~C. R. E.~~

83RD FIELD COY R.E.
JLY 1915 – MAY 1919

121/6300

20th Division

83rd F.C. R.E.
Vol. I.

Jan 22 - 30-4-15

May '15

Army Form C. 2118.

83rd F.C. R.E.

WAR DIARY
or
INTELLIGENCE SUMMARY
(Erase heading not required.)

Place	Date	Hour	Summary of Events and Information	Remarks and references to Appendices
Larkhill	22/7 15	3 am	Left for Amesbury Station. Entrainment.	
Southampton		7 am	arrived. Entrained transport & horses & car/cart. Let others & they sailed for Havre about 3 p.m. Remember ironclads worked, as the ship could not proceed on account of bad weather.	
"	23.7		Major Hopkins CO + 3 Officers + Lieutenants branch of company marched up to rest camp at Southampton. Consumed 3 pm an available.	
"	24.7		Paraded at Rest Camp. 3/30 pm & embarked at 5/30 on S.S. Connaught - sailed for Havre about 6 pm with details of R.F.A. + Reg. Cyps + 61 + 62 Ambulance. Major Hopkins in command of troops. Arrived Havre 11 pm	
Le Havre	25.7		Disembarked 6 am and marched to No 5 Camp to join mounted portion whole arrived at railway station Pt 2 at 9/30 + Entrained. Train left at 1/30 pm	

Army Form C. 2118.

WAR DIARY
or
INTELLIGENCE SUMMARY.
(Erase heading not required.)

Place	Date	Hour	Summary of Events and Information	Remarks and references to Appendices
	25.7	—	Proceeding by train via Rouen, Abancourt, apparently Calais St Omer.	
St Omer	26.7	7am	at Omer ordered to detrain at Lumbres. Reached Lumbres at 8/30 detrained & marched off at 10/30 am arrived at BOISDINGHEM at 12/30. Sundries in barns. Officers in ruin Houses + horse pickets in a field. Weather very fine.	
BOISDINGHEM	27.7		Halt. Dismounted men went for route march & ground exercise. C.O. went to divl HQrs in morning. Returned today. Lumbers arriv	
	28.7		marched off at 10/15 am en route to Argues. Halted to water & fed at NIEURLET arrived Argues 2pm, handed in 5 mile 24 road map + billets in Fort Rouge for men car + 2 officers. Remainder bivouacd in a field. 20 officers in small unfurnished room in tenement	

W. Elliot Major

Army Form C. 2118.

WAR DIARY
or
INTELLIGENCE SUMMARY
(Erase heading not required.)

Place	Date	Hour	Summary of Events and Information	Remarks and references to Appendices
PRADELLES	29.7		Marched at 9.45 am. proceeded to PRADELLES via Ebblinghem & Hazebrouck arrived PRADELLES at 3/30 pm. having halts to water horses at Wallon cappel 35 min + at Sotterage 10 min for ations. information to water & feed bivouaced in a grass field. Some rain. beer & few at night	
OULTERSTEEN	30.7		Marched off at 8/20 am. with remainder of 60 Bde to OULTERSTEENE arrived there 10/30 am. Men what marched caused drivers who bivouac in field behind with the horses. Officers in fort billets. after some delay, my front Col de Jun. manoeuvres chn both their trumpets & under CRE orders made the Williamson Oddetta white to improve water supply. Lt. 5 pm t returned 9 & 9 pm	Waymouth

131/6754

20th Burman

83rd L.C.R.E.
Vol. II

August 15.

WAR DIARY
INTELLIGENCE SUMMARY

83rd Co. R.E.

Army Form C. 2118

Place	Date	Hour	Summary of Events and Information	Remarks and references to Appendices
OULTER STEENE	15 31·7		Company moved by road Boipul in to new billets at farmhouse near Merris.	
MERRIS	1/8		Improving water supply of various units.	
D⁰	2/8/15		1 & 3 sections went to Pont Neuve with pontoon & will began work on a bridge but there were orders of 26th Division Co. 2nd section's improving water supply & other small works to division.	
D⁰	3/8		Commenced work on sinking wells at New Berquin Kitchen & Company huts. Wheeling bricks at Farbus and sand & cement to Steyville. Work hindered by non arrival of lorries ordered & difficulty in getting view of cement lorries & brick lorries by C.R. & CRE of the Division. Whole are lorries all suffer to-day owing...	

Army Form C. 2118

5/

83rd C.O.R.E.

WAR DIARY
or
INTELLIGENCE SUMMARY.

(Erase heading not required.)

Instructions regarding War Diaries and Intelligence Summaries are contained in F.S. Regs., Part II. and the Staff Manual respectively. Title pages will be prepared in manuscript.

Place	Date	Hour	Summary of Events and Information	Remarks and references to Appendices
ADS			Work continues on wells & arrangements for having temporary huts for guest room & offices in which there is no room in the billets.	
7.8.15 MERRIS			Work on 30 yard rifle range commenced into infantry working parties. Two in 6th Brigade area & 1 in each of other brigade area transports in charge of former & Co. + kitchen set out at one at Secque Cookers started the 55ft range. Men are well contented.	

1577 Wt. W10791/1773 500,000 1/15 D. D. & L. A.D.S.S./Forms/C. 2118.

WAR DIARY or INTELLIGENCE SUMMARY

Army Form C. 2118

83rd Co. R.E.

Place	Date	Hour	Summary of Events and Information	Remarks and references to Appendices
MERRIS	8/8/15		Hants working parties on ranges in afternoon & Sappers working on wells. Major & Spain went to St Omer by motor to prepare list of bridges in Devaux area. Information obtained at Hazebrouck from District Engineer & subsequently checked on the spot.	
do	9.8.15		Hants working parties on the ranges & horseshoe ellance in the morning. 94th C.O. orders and sent by wire to report to OC Field Cos. Hinecourt RE with 1 + 3 sections for instruction in trenches.	
BAC ST MAUR	10.8.15		Marched off at 3 am. & arrived BAC ST MAUR 6·25 am. Billets not yet vacant - men bivouacs till vacated at 10 am. Major Wilson made tour of trenches into OC 157 Co + Gallipoli & Armentieres with 2nd Field Co. at night	

Army Form C. 2118

WAR DIARY
or
INTELLIGENCE SUMMARY.
(Erase heading not required.)

83rd Co. R.E.

Place	Date	Hour	Summary of Events and Information	Remarks and references to Appendices
BAC ST MAUR	11.8		Capt Scott & 1 section attached to No 2 Field Amb. Major McPherson A.D.M.S. & McBredon attached to No 5 Field Co. for instruction	
	12.8		Officers inspected works in winter day & night & men more employed constructing and obstacles & conducting entry. Working parties on new Communication trenches	
	13.8		Major McPherson inspected the Home Counties Engineer works & to be taken over by No 1 & 3 sections	
	14.8		Men at working in trenches day & night. O.C. inspected the communications trenches made by No 4 section.	
	15.8			
	16.8		No 3 & 1 sections relieved & moved to B.A.C. St MAUR & completed the hedge head defences begun from week No 2 & 4 sections returned to RUE DEZ ALYS to work on posts near LAVENTIE. Moved to new billets in afternoon, raining all day	Movements map 18.8.15
	17.8			

WAR DIARY
or
INTELLIGENCE SUMMARY

Army Form C. 2118

83 Field Co RE

Place	Date	Hour	Summary of Events and Information	Remarks and references to Appendices
RwE Nela SYS.	18.8	—	Commenced work on improved ESQUIN. FORT	
Do	19.8	—	Taken over works. Party started work on slated meaning plan of support line posts between PETILLON & FAUQUISSART	
Do	20.8	—	Taken over Laventie Sand Pits. Pt 100 Infantry on fatigue Pont d'epiny	
Do	21.8	—	Commenced trench work in rear. Stopped work on Laventie Support line Posts by order of Division, alleged to be under observation of Hostile trench workmen on Laventie North Fort. Examined sites for enemy Cement M.G. emplacements in front line NW of 59th Bty M.G. Officer	
Do	22.8	—	Continued work on improvement of Fort. Hat on Laventie to date. Sunday no work done. Fineday. Several cases of mild diarrhoea & vomiting among Lieut officers and men. Seems among in street area. 3 men in hospital with "influenza". These very bad weather. Due to dirty-crowded midden in farm building.	
FD.	23.8	—	Continued improving Laventie N & E forts. Begun & making roads & preparing frames nautical for Cement M.G. emplacements only. 70 infants working party available. Given a Blm Long from No. Ben Park Weich Fend & Armenters for trucks etc. Employed in forwarding parts for wire entanglement from Laventie Ironmonger. A quantity of sparks fencing posts for wire entanglements	

1577 Wt.W10791/1773 500,000 1/15 D. D. & L. A.D.S.S./Forms/C. 2118.

WAR DIARY
INTELLIGENCE SUMMARY

Army Form C.2118

83 2nd C.
R.E.

Place	Date	Hour	Summary of Events and Information	Remarks and references to Appendices
Rue de la Lys	24th Aug	Monday	Working improvements to huts. First portion of Coy. which was supplemented into M.G. Officer 83 Brigade & hts of Loophole sent up some cement & sandbags.	
"	25th	Tues	Went round the present known line into O.C. 4 & 5th Company from taking them over on 29th. Lieutenants & 9 men blew up a sniper post between our lines & the German at night. No casualties.	
"	26th	Thurs	Continued work on improving the huts & making out roads.	
LAVENTIE	27th	Friday	HqBn & 2nd section moved to billets in Laventie, arriving 8/pm. Continued to Laventie. 5th to 6th O.E.S. Et. Collecting materials & expects want round left-half front. O.C. inspected right-half in afternoon.	
"	28th	Saturday	At 8pm. started to putup 300 men to improve the stopped reserve trenches. They worked all night. Very little firing. Some rain about 1am. Heavy dew.	
"	29th		250 infantry working under R.E. improve breastwork. 1-3 section joined the Company from B.H.Q. at M.Q.R. orders the Convoy afternoon at this would be abandoned meantime from 2am. There was something out to be done, which interfered with work but he could hope.	

Army Form C. 2118

10

WAR DIARY
INTELLIGENCE SUMMARY.
83rd Field Co. R.E.

(Erase heading not required.)

Instructions regarding War Diaries and Intelligence Summaries are contained in F. S. Regs., Part II. and the Staff Manual respectively. Title pages will be prepared in manuscript.

Place	Date	Hour	Summary of Events and Information	Remarks and references to Appendices
LAVENTIE	30th		Working parties improving support & reserve trenches with torpedoes. — Repairing.	
	31st		Infantry 6 killed working party killed by a rifle. Support trenches shelled but no casualty. Working parties improving support & reserve trenches. OC went round trenches. Several in trenches. Only broken parties in	

Wauchope
Major R.E.

28th Kinnear

6371/14

S₃ of F.C.R.E.
Vol. III
Sept. 15

Army Form C. 2118.

WAR DIARY
or
INTELLIGENCE SUMMARY.
(Erase heading not required.)

83 Field Coy RE

Place	Date	Hour	Summary of Events and Information	Remarks and references to Appendices
LAVENTIE	Sep 1		Infantry working parties improving the trenches & communication Dtls. Work stopped by order of Brigadier on account of gun in evening.	
	2		Minimum was working parties. OC. went round before dark.	
	3		Working parties debout upon night very thick. OC went front by trenches.	
	4			
	5		Minimum day parties. OC. went round right side. Weather full of rain for last three days & walking very heavy. 250 men were on wire at night in report trenches.	
	6.		Work in trenches continued with infantry working parties. Parties were out checked & 2 other killed + 3 wounded	
	7. & 8.		Work continued. Company A.H.O.L. found out & started the names & numbers the right front trenches.	

Recamalle on working parties for supporting bills
[signature] to section of W/o. M [signature]
1577 Wt. W10791/P773 500,000 1/15 D.D.&L. A.D.S.S./Forms/C. 2118. Sept 9. 1915

WAR DIARY
INTELLIGENCE SUMMARY

(Erase heading not required.)

Army Form C. 2118.

Place	Date	Hour	Summary of Events and Information	Remarks and references to Appendices
LAVENTIE	9.9.15		Work continued on dugouts, trenches & sallyports. Weather fine. Average daily issue of sandbags for the brigade 10,000, ten thousand - timber enough for 25 dugouts pr 6. Barbed wire about 1 mile & pickets. 4 wagon loads of Revettris 50 to front every night - this is exclusive of artillery requirement which they draw direct from OME	
	10-12		Working on dugouts & trenches	
LAVENTIE	13. Sept		Same work continued. Reserve trench fourth shelled & sappers driven in. Support line hitton hard by rifles.	
Do	14 Sept		Sappers withdrew hurd on trench line habited. Sapper Hawke hit by shrapnell in reserve trenches & died in trenches hospital same day.	

WAR DIARY
or
INTELLIGENCE SUMMARY.
(Erase heading not required.)

Army Form C. 2118.

83 Field Coy R.E.

Place	Date	Hour	Summary of Events and Information	Remarks and references to Appendices
LAVENTIE	15/9/15		Constructing dugouts, taking up large quantities of material for these, repairing the covered tramways & putting in sidings.	
	16/9		Reveille at night & working parties.	
	17/9		Reveille at night & working parties by day. Sappers getting tram ways in order & getting out work for night.	
	18/9 to 24/9		Working on construction of dugouts in the support, assembly & reserve trenches for 6th Brigade. Some shelling. Sapper T. Martin & Sapper Valentine wounded on 22nd. Weather fine till 23rd when heavy rain came on. Night & evening at 5 p.m. company paraded & marched off to the trenches. No 1 & 2 Sections to the assembly trenches between WINCHESTER STREET & WINCHESTER ROAD. No 3 to ELGIN STATION ASSEMBLY trenches & No 4 into OCt W 8 p & Road Bend Post.	[signature]

WAR DIARY or INTELLIGENCE SUMMARY

Army Form C. 2118.

Place	Date	Hour	Summary of Events and Information	Remarks and references to Appendices
near CHAPIGNY FARM	Sept 25 15		Stores of wire & pickets & tools were previously collected at CHAPLIN & ELGIN CRATERS & the 1, 2, 3 sections spent some hours of the night preparing for attack. They all turned (4) stood to arms at 4/30 am but the attack had been postponed one hour and No 1 section which had the job of wiring the trench which the infantry were to dig across to the German lines at pt 76 did not get to work till 6/30 am. They laid out two coils of French wire 90 yds long while the infantry formed up sand bags & tried to dig a trench without much success. As parapet was hit by heavy trench mortars. Sappers were killed & two wounded & about 30 engaged. The section retired when the infantry were driven in. Cockran & McLachlan attacked the German line about 9/30 am into the (2 R.Brigade this reminded on their line some & heavier having found them without difficulty) They were hurried out by a feeble counterattack as they had not prepared for defence. It seems very that a fire step was necessary to make them to fire over the parapets & the communication trench required flooring. He tries to get them to do those works but the discussion the men to like sheep incapable of concentrated effort and attempt by continued messages to about them "downle" which they had been known to from along by word of mouth to they	

WAR DIARY or INTELLIGENCE SUMMARY

Army Form C. 2118.

83 Field Amb[ulance]

Place	Date	Hour	Summary of Events and Information	Remarks and references to Appendices
	25th Sept 15		Three men of No 2 section with the bearers up the hurdles finally lost their lives when hit by enemy bombers in the return across the open. They (McLaine) many casualties. No 2 section had three men wounded & three others slightly wounded. McL[aine] wounded was abandoned killed with 20 others at the Dressing Station. No 2 section was attached to the 12th R.B. who did not engage. No 4 Section was employed bringing up ammunition from Rouge Bank Fort which they did near the French Chaplain station in three trips during the work. Seven were knocked down by H.E. shell. Kempf, Peplan being severely injured & dying before reaching the advanced dressing station. Sergt Pain took charge of No 1 Section & about 4 p.m. alarm orders were issued on to return to ambulance posts & at 6 p.m. orders were issued on to return to Billets in Rue de Paradis, Laventie. Collecting tools & equipment. At night 1.3.4 sections prepared during relations engagement. No 2 section went to FLEURBAY 3 miles to gain from RUETILLEROY up to the Front Parapet. No 24 to	
LAVENTIE	26th			

Westland
Major

Army Form C. 2118.

WAR DIARY
or
INTELLIGENCE SUMMARY.
(Erase heading not required.)

83 Field Coy RE

Place	Date	Hour	Summary of Events and Information	Remarks and references to Appendices
LAVENTIE	Sept 26/15		Being warned for an attack on following morning this was cancelled & they returned to billets at 12 midnight.	
"	27th		Nieuwgram — work kept repairing railways & collecting stores etc.	
"	28th		Took over the new on right & also some dump alongside front.	
"	29th		Nieuwgram went round new trenches which crews were on his	
"	30th		Party had everywhere. Started connecting up the old hundred ant making trench boards & railway track as fast as possible.	

[signature]
Major R.E.
O.C. 83rd ? Co R.E.

30/9/15

Operation order N°7.
by
Major R.E. Hopkins R.E.
C/o #3 Field Co.

Map. 1/10000 sheet 36 S.W.1.

(1) Operations — The Meerut Division on our right will attack the German trenches in front of them with the ultimate object of obtaining possession of the high ground between Haut Pommereau & La Cliquetrie farm.
Map Ref. T1 to T3.
The attack will be at   oclock on Sept.
The 20th Divn will co-operate with them & as the Meerut Divn establishes itself in advance ~~according to the success of the Meerut attack~~ ~~the operation of the~~ 60th Brigade will ~~be~~ push forward ~~confined~~ to an immediate objective followed by a more extended movement carrying the attack up to AUBERS & beyond.

(2) Objective — The first objective of the 60th Brigade will be to establish itself on the line connecting the saphead at M24 c61 with the left of the Meerut Division at the point 476 in the German trenches.
Having made good here the second objective is the German front & support trenches between point 476 & 61. on map.
The third point to be made is the house at N19 c 2½ 3. & the communication trench SW of Rue d'Enfer.

Disposition   The Meerut division occupies our front line up to
              M 24. C 72 &   remainder by
              1 & 2 Batt⁰ⁿ hold the front line.

              N° 4 Batt⁰ⁿ will assemble in the support
              & assembly trenches Winchester Street to Lonely
              Sap.

              N° 3 Batt⁰ⁿ will hold the reserve line
              Winchester to Elgin Street & the reserve
              posts. Winchester to Marselot.

              Ad⁰ Q⁰ⁿ N° 1 & 4 Batt⁰ⁿ behind Chaplen dam
                          3 — on Reserve line Elgin Street
                                                   Junction.

              The 83 Field Co. 1 & 2 sections will occupy
                   an auxty
              their trench between Chaplen dam & Winchester
              Street. 3 section at Elgin St⁰ & H⁰ Q⁰s
              & 4 section at Road Bend. Transport at
              Rue de Paradis. 40 men of N° 3 Batt⁰ⁿ
                      will be attached as a carrying party at
              Advanced stores of the following Chaplen & 40 at Elgin
                                              have been formed
              at Chaplen Station & Elgin Station.

              French wire   100 rolls   50 coils
              & staples.
              Barbed wire   200 coils   100 coils
              plain wire   10 coils   5 coils.
              Long pickets   200   100
              Short pickets 200   100
              Chevaux de frise 100   50.
              Billhooks   10   5 —
              Shovels   100   100
              Picks   50   50.
              Hurdles   20.   10.

Operations. No 21 batln will hold the saphead & extends the sap passing up filled sandbags for this purpose & they will send a patrol round by Winchester road to work back from point 76 ~~to meet~~ the saphead.

~~No 1~~ Section R.E. will collect 20 coils of trench wire at the Sap & be prepared to lay it out to protect the sap down to point 76. The operation will be screened by smoke bombs sent over by the trench Mortar battery. They will take a carrying party of 20 ~~of the~~ attackers Inf.

Wounded. Company Stretcher ~~will~~ be with No 1 section.
4 Batt~~Dressing Stations~~ ~~motor Dressyrstations~~ at East end of Chaplin St.
2 — ? Bedford Road
1 — bet Chaplin St & S Elgin St.

Mot aid Post. at Chaplin Farm. + No 2 Bath H.Qrs.
Walking cases will evacuate by Lonely Path & Mancelot Street which are reserve for down traffic. Other cases will be evacuated by tramway on the tracks marked for the purpose which will be handed over to B'st ambulance by No 1 + 3 section officers.

Communication will be from front to rear.

Communication. 1 & B section must keep CO informed of their movements. By telephone from Chaplin Farm Hd Qrs or by runner.

Equipment.

Each man will carry. 100 rounds ammunt.
filled water bottle.
ration in haversack.
Pack containing iron ration
waterproof sheet
Jersey,
socks,
mess tin.

+ each section will carry.
axes felling   5.
Hammers claw   5
Saws hand.   1
Billhooks   10
Shovels   10
Picks   5.
Guncotton   25 lbs arranged on boards in 5 & 10 lb charges.
wire cutters. Each mate.

The section tool carts forage carts + pack animals will remain at Rue de Paradis ready to move. They + the Hd Qrs transport will be in charge of Capt Scott who will keep in touch with the telephone at Brigade Hd Qrs.

Bicycles: will be taken to assembly posts. Each section will hand over two to HdQrs for their use to S Major by 10 am 20th.

Bridging wagons will carry the trestles & following stores
9 × 3   15 baulks.   15ft long.
9 × 6   10   15ft long.
4½ × 3   100 ft
3/p° bolts   100
dogs   100
6" nails   50 lbs

Surplus kits & blankets to be packed by 10am on 20th & stacked on the guard room at Rue de Paradis
Each section will so tag & mark together their own kits & blankets.

Rations & Water will be delivered to ~~Squares~~ RE Store & Baker Street by RQMS & fetched from there by sections.

Ad. position will be at Road Bend ~~near the~~ Advanced Brigade Support Centre at M ~~#20~~ 17 d 4 6.

Operations for 2nd & 3rd Objectives.

After No 4 Battn & Meerut Divn have
captured their first objective, a
further advance against the enemy's
trenches between point 76 & 61 connecting
with the advance of Meerut Divn
No 4 Battn will attack in lines of
half companies. No 3 will carry
on the work of entrenching from Saphead
M 24 c 61 to point 76 assisted by No 1 section
No 1 section will make chevaux de frise to prepare a
No 1 & 2 section will advance in rear strong line of defence here.
of the 2nd half of 2nd Company of No 4
Battn carrying wire & chevaux de frise
their role will be to cut wire remove
obstacles & cut mine & telephone wires.
Me will take 30 men after infantry as
carrying party.

As the advance continues No 1 Battn
will attack on left of No 4 Battn.
They start with trenches with their right
on M 24 d 38. & the right of their attack
is pt 55. on gaining the German trenches
they will work along communication trench
to point 09. 36. 33.
No 3 section 83 Co will follow No 3 Co.
moving up by S & L been opened.

orders. will be sent for the advance of No 1 Batt.
& No 2 section will detail an orderly or signaller
~~to meet~~ with No 3 Co of No 1 Batt. and will move
off ~~behind~~ them when they advance

The infantry carrying parties with them will
bring up chevaux de frise wire & barbed
wire. staples picks & shovels.

Sappers carrying wire cutters ought to have
a piece of white tape attached to their
backs for any indentification

121.
7517

30th Division

83rd F.C. R.E.
Vol. 4

Col 15

Army Form C. 2118.

WAR DIARY
or
INTELLIGENCE SUMMARY.
(Erase heading not required.)

83rd Field Ambulance

Place	Date	Hour	Summary of Events and Information	Remarks and references to Appendices
LAVENTIE	May/15 6 7th		Wet cell + trench fatigue mud. Working on trench gangways opened + extension of tramway. Prepared to make a smoke demonstration on 5th but storm postponed. Drawing water from front line was considered + attempt as an experiment to see what would be required.	
	8th		On the 8th there was a call for 1000 sandbags to repair the front line (damaged by mine + into night Lectice Spencer between the Rifle + fusilier trenches in wooden boxes carried out-ration efforts of stretcher bearers in wooden boxes conducted with sand + shrub by the electric detonators for forward smoke	
	9th		The smoke demonstration again postponed + performance taken on again at night by NCO's parties. One box charges removed by Germans.	
	10 F to 11.		Pts Ja. Lumbir Softer Harvey killed by M.G. fire near trenches in ours & with line being erected for kitchen on reserve trench. Boundary information + drainage scheme stated to be well water from trenches by fatigue	

1577 Wt.W10791/1773 500,000 1/15 D. D. & L. A.D.S.S./Forms/C. 2118.

		Army Form C. 2118.
		83 Field Co RE

WAR DIARY
or
INTELLIGENCE SUMMARY.
(Erase heading not required.)

Place	Date	Hour	Summary of Events and Information	Remarks and references to Appendices
LAVENTIE	12/3/15		Return stores placed out between the lines about 100 lbs of ammonphos Phosphorus in 16 groups, 16 woodentroughs containing tin to each & fired by electric detonators from the Parapet. Each group lit two circuits, to allow for failures. None of these were caught fire during next morning, & at 12/30 pm (the wind) being favourable for all except the left group, all circuits of each group were fired & the execution about 1/15 pm & smoke was then drifting till 2 p.m. along the whole 400 thgds front. There was much shelling by the Germans and the demonstration closed by 2/30 pm. There were no RE casualties.	Murphy Major RE
"	13th			
	14th 16 18th		Clearing out trench & collecting tramways. Conveyance manage to trenches was done by wheeled & supplies were employed to relieve systematically, if position of sappers, each who intends parties took up the work.	

Army Form C. 2118.

(19)

83 Co RE

WAR DIARY
or
INTELLIGENCE SUMMARY.
(Erase heading not required.)

Instructions regarding War Diaries and Intelligence Summaries are contained in F. S. Regs., Part II. and the Staff Manual respectively. Title pages will be prepared in manuscript.

Place	Date	Hour	Summary of Events and Information	Remarks and references to Appendices
LAVENTIE	19 to 21.		Winter hutting continued cleaning of relics	
	22		All four shafts the company employed on construction earthworks near shelters for fractionary troop in the attack	
	23 & 24		20 trunks at salaires being carried on & hutting & tramway complete with staff front up to the front line near Chapelin Farm (Chaplains) & found up with line to wounded group. Heavy rain & little work done	
	25.		Some rain but work progressing	
	26 & 27		Lt Mainwaring attached to 96 Co on 27th to replace Harrison killed. Heavy rain again flows the ditches & mud antholes everywhere. The work almost untouched	
	28		Commenced revetting Winchester C. Trench	
	29.			
	30.		Ordered to make a new parapet 200 yds long in front of line near Bucket Hd	
	31.		Parapet made 4ft high revetted with fascines & 2ft thick at top. Working parties of 1050 men & 120 sappers. No casualties. Wet weather through Knowlestones) are in front.	

1577 Wt. W1079/1773 500,000 1/15 D.D. & L. A.D.S.S./Forms/C. 2118.

83rd F.C.R.E.
vol. 5

121/7624

20th Division

Nov 15.

WAR DIARY or INTELLIGENCE SUMMARY

Army Form C. 2118

83 A'6 R5

Place	Date	Hour	Summary of Events and Information	Remarks and references to Appendices
LAVENTIE	Nov 1/15		Work on new parapet at Dead-dog continued with 750 men. enemy's two trench trains for the purpose owing to bad weather, fitful daylight & working parties not returning at the time specified. little work has been done. In this division the French are under the orders of the Brigade Commander but the result that the Sappers become a pawn & have little control over work done. The R.E. are continually interfering with + no progress is made. The wooden revetting frames proved a great success about 30 completed & two sappers can turn out 100-8/5 frames per day. They are carried by two men, can be set up in correct position by any one. Give the correct angle & slope & are far better than 6 times greater than sand bagging or protecting. The infantry clearly have easily completed a 4'6" breastwork W/6 thick at top with first night with traverses but neither officers nor men take any trouble. The revett in that and is dragged in over twice the time & sappers get fed up & get all the ...	

WAR DIARY
or
INTELLIGENCE SUMMARY.

Army Form C. 2118.

(Erase heading not required.)

Place	Date	Hour	Summary of Events and Information	Remarks and references to Appendices
Laventie	Nov 2.		Parapets (Ship & hrs working parties). Margarine containers and the parapets and Communication trenches are collapsing everywhere. Sand bag revetment lost about 2 men hrs in the wounds of it is built in by bit brick into a depth of 4 and not more than 5 courses high. Revetting of sub-communication trenches not broken and revetment picketis 4½"x3" – 6,7,8 ft apart with two tangents 5x2" behind wire & canvas pushed behind – canvas is essential – the lot is inclined back and the top should come to the top at least. Frame about 12" above bottom of trench. Others on hand the trench ½ a Company RE & 150 infantry can do about 50 yds a day.	
	Nov 3.		Work continued on dicks Bill machine gun fairly noisy mainly ASTANCE + 2 officers prolonged. Infantry difficult to get out to the horror but + 500 men difficult to induce to work it serves repairs he had a dr in the infantry officers were kept any work done. WMcRae Knott Man Mkt	

Army Form C. 2118.

83 Field Coy RE

WAR DIARY
or
INTELLIGENCE SUMMARY
(Erase heading not required.)

Place	Date	Hour	Summary of Events and Information	Remarks and references to Appendices
AVENTIE	4/XI/15	5.	Lt Maunder returned to duty with Co. & took over Duck's Bill work on which worked 375 men. Employed.	
		6.	Party pumping out Communication trenches. 375 men on Duck's Bill new parapet.	
		7.	400 men on Duck's Bill parapet.	
		8.	Sunday no work in day time. Major Hopkins went up South Maroc Street trenches front. Shot to find west end to the front. Very heavy men in C.T. 877 infantry working parties to-day. 350 on Duck's Bill. 74 on Winchester Street working. 140 Company trench bottoms to front line & 200 cleaning out Communication trenches.	
		9.	Weather wet & packs bothered by shelling. Islands have taken 18 Receipts to do. Receipt of 45 casks of creosote. 7 English to do 2 nights easy work. This is not altogether the result of bad weather & machine gun fire. Much pumping & musketeering. 200 men work on Duck's Bill rid army to team.	
	10th		Lieut. on S Tilley St. & Mentes Frange. Improvements.	Maunder

Army Form C. 2118.

WAR DIARY
or
INTELLIGENCE SUMMARY.
(Erase heading not required.)

83 Field Co RE

Place	Date	Hour	Summary of Events and Information	Remarks and references to Appendices
Laventie	11		Much rain + little work done.	
	12			
	13			
	14		Relieved by 55 Co RE & Guards Brigade in reserve repairing posts in rear etc	
	15			
	16			
	17			
	18		Taking over from 15 Co RE which the trenches between Cellar Farm + Cordonnerie with the CO of 1/5 Co. very heavy rain all day. C/Practice Pastols works + trenchine work CO of 2nd Fusiliers who hands over part to this Coy. 2nd Fitzgerald + No 4 Section marched to Rue d'Enmer at 9.30 am to take over the White + papier.	
	19			
	20		Company marched to Rue d'Enmer at 6/30 am & arrived at 10/30am CO reported to Brigadier + then took over...(arrow) trenches	
BHQ St M[...]Rd	21			

Wurrfield
Captain

Army Form C. 2118.

WAR DIARY
or
INTELLIGENCE SUMMARY.
(Erase heading not required.)

8rd Fd Co R.E.

Place	Date	Hour	Summary of Events and Information	Remarks and references to Appendices
BAC ST MAUR	22/11/15 23rd		8th Division still in our trenches. Our Sappers working in front line & in Tin Barn Avenue. Improving of workshop accommodation taken inhand & clearing up the billet.	
	24th		62nd Fd Coy RE took over the area from 8th Divn. Company work as follows. 3rd section in front line 2 sect. on Communications. 1 section in rearpark & headquarter work. 2 men per section assembled in workshop at Hd Qrs & 2 on lathring. Also working 10 French Carpenters + 20 inf'y pioneers on billets, also HQ inf'y pioneers attached for fatigue duties loading, unloading & carrying engineering work.	
	25th		Cold & frosty night. Lt Rutjens employed constructed to CRE fm 28th Dec during absence Lt Maori.	
	26th		Both hands at ordinary Company employed near Headquarters, which was returned to be to front line.	
	27th		Sunday. Return to front line & pray.	
	28th		Hard frost. Several two hands for dugout. C.O. received City road to improving the drainage. Capt Yorke wounded by sniper while out of the trench at loft of City road.	
	29th			
	30th Jan		1 & 2 section employed in front line with 2 section infantry pioneers – moved to billets near Mons Farm. So as to be nearer their work.	

Army Form C. 2118.

WAR DIARY
or
INTELLIGENCE SUMMARY

83rd Da. Co. R.E.

(Erase heading not required.)

Place	Date	Hour	Summary of Events and Information	Remarks and references to Appendices
BAC ST. MAUR	1/12/15		Section working in improving front parapet from Dunn avenue to Dead Tree and revetting communication trenches.	
	4/xii		1 Section with 21 Platoon Pioneers returning North. avenue revetting.	
	5/xii		Search lights were used without him to keeping enemys wire + parapet aft. bombardment during day. Bayonets of rifles were rung to the distance post - front - + nr=enemy showing infants of parapet.	
	6/xii		River kept rising rapidly + floods(?) and the magazine where ? ammo mined to higher ground during the day. Some powder was lost.	
	10.xii		Thanks of the 3rd Corps Commander received for the excellent state of the trenches which we handed over to the Guards Divn - these were mainly in the 88rd C. charge.	
	11-15		Heavy rain + floods which drowned out all communication trenches + covered the ground around billets inches deep - up to the knee deep throwing out some c little + all the billeting underhips.	
	16F.		River kept + floods mined retired company in reserve fourth 16th Dec. with 65 th Brigade	

Army Form C. 2118.
26

WAR DIARY
or
INTELLIGENCE SUMMARY.
(Erase heading not required.)

83rd Fd Co R E

Place	Date	Hour	Summary of Events and Information	Remarks and references to Appendices
BAC ST NAZR	17		Company working on various small works in reserve area & in hutting. Weather mild & not much rain. Flood subsided considerably.	
	18			
	21.			
	22.		huts.	
	23.			
	24.		Went into ng bt brigade area. Border to Devon Avenue.	
	25.		Examining new trenches for work. M8 d55 b N10 b 5.10. Shots seen again & Rbgs up &	
	26.		the Roadway at Breitmaur	
	27.		4 mns 2 & 7 pumps put up in Calen Run communication trench, but little improvem made in its role till too men had been put to pumps, when the	
	28.		floods began to subside & water was quickly got out of Cruikshank anything	
	29.		for a both sides. Causing a few casualties but not passage to trenches	
	30.			
	31.		Heavy gale & general thawing	

Signed
Major R.E.
O/C 83 Fd Co
Jan 1st

63rd F.C.R.E.
Vol: 7

Army Form C. 2118.

(27)

83rd Field C.R.E.

WAR DIARY
INTELLIGENCE SUMMARY
(Erase heading not required.)

Place	Date	Hour	Summary of Events and Information	Remarks and references to Appendices
A&C ST MAUR	1/1/16 to 10/1/16		Two sections working in Front Line from Devon Avenue N10 to Bond Street N8 M St. improving parapet & traverses, making new traverses, relaying trench boards in traffic trench. One section working on Cellar Farm + V.C. Avenues, maintenance of Cellar Farm + V.C. Railways, resetting fortified Post. Hutting carried on, also work on Corduroy roads, Stables for HQ &c. Occurrences during this period. 3.1.16 Sapper Will G wounded. 5.1.16 2nd Cpl R n Purvis killed by Stray bullet. 7.1.16 Sapt Barendale N wounded. Two motor pumps installed in Cellar Farm Avenue. 8.1.16 Advance party proceeded to new rest area to take over billets.	
	11/1/16		Company marched to Grand See Bois where it was billetted for the night. 2nd Lt Sebon with 6 men remain behind to clean up and handover billets to 2nd Field Co R.E.	
STEENBECQUE	12/1/16		Company marched to new area + billetted at Steenbecque. 2nd Lt Sebon & party rejoined here.	
	13/1/16 to 20/1/16		Company in rest area fitting work, squad & company drill, field works, improvements to billets + preparation of road signs &c.	
"	21/1/16		Company paraded for inspection + address by III Corps Commander in recognition of their leaving the Corps. Thanked for excellent work done while with III Corps.	

M G W... M R E
Capt
O C 83 F Co R E

WAR DIARY
INTELLIGENCE SUMMARY

Army Form C. 2118.

83rd Field Co. R.E.

Place	Date	Hour	Summary of Events and Information	Remarks and references to Appendices
STEENBECQUE	22/7/16		Company marched to join VIth Corps Billets at P.24 a 7.4.	
Billets at P.24 a 7.4	23/7/16 to 30/7/16		Company resting in billets. Work, company request drill, rifle & musketry exercises, practising with smoke helmets, pontoon bridging, field works & demolitions. On 30/7/16 2nd Lt Mainwaring left the company to join 84th Field Co. R.E. on transfer. 2/Lt Watson R.E. joined the company from 84th Field Co. R.E. on transfer.	
"	31/7/16		Company marched past G.O.C. II Army.	

M.A. H[?]
Capt. R.E.
O.C. 83rd Field Co. R.E.

Army Form C. 2118

WAR DIARY
or
INTELLIGENCE SUMMARY
(Erase heading not required.)

83rd Field Co R.E.

Place	Date	Hour	Summary of Events and Information	Remarks and references to Appendices
ST SYLVESTRE CAPPEL	Feb. 1		2/Lt Bagnall + Capt Kilgallen went to the 14th Div H.Qrs. by bus with other officers to be taken round the new area of trenches which we are to work at/to relieving 14th Divn. afsets of 14 Engrs. from the C. was transferred to Coulomby hut in the new forward area. Company and no horses will be placed by full mrs. + for lorry.	
	2		Sent 84 to Inniskillens mustered to attack + bought back our positions from the 84 To. The company went to recent watch from the hasty turbulence, I am not. But the country remains sodden and muddy.	
	3		Twelve hundred light bulbs partitioning mendevdeer emitted on maintained hoofed without delay and wellop toward into must we repeat redirect which some may intakes + new T.M. huts in reserve and hitherto bend net	
	4		Earthwork completed + afterwards destroyed the German a German 87.9 gun and 8ft high Caula destroyed in 15 mirror by placing two tins by charge of 5 mirror ten	

Army Form C. 2118.

30

83 Field Coy.

WAR DIARY
or
INTELLIGENCE SUMMARY

(Erase heading not required.)

Place	Date	Hour	Summary of Events and Information	Remarks and references to Appendices
ST SYLVESTRE CAPPEL	5 Feb.		Fixed + began about 18 ms at the corner where the funeral passes to Chapel. This charge is ample.	
			Marched to WATOU	
WATOU 6 Feb			Billets in 5 Farms - one mile west of the village.	
	7 Feb.		Made a 65 yd rifle range with 5 targets.	
	8 Feb.		2 sections fired 5 rounds rapid practice. 2 went into much of next to PEYPAERTS + on the WORMHOUT to confer with Fields Commander 61st & 62nd F.C. manoeuvre + returned to WATOU in afternoon.	
	9 Feb.		Remainder 6 fired rapid practice. O.C. again went to VLAMERTINGHE + at night went round the trenches with officers of 62 F.C. 2nd Lt. WATSON went with him.	
	10 Feb.		O.C. moved to new Camp near ELVERDIMGHE and 2nd Lt WATSON took advanced party to Headqrs on the Canal bank + took up work and dugouts there.	

W.Watkins
Capt. RE
OC 83 Field Coy RE

Army Form C. 2118.

WAR DIARY
or
INTELLIGENCE SUMMARY.

(Erase heading not required.)

83 Field Co R.E.

Place	Date	Hour	Summary of Events and Information	Remarks and references to Appendices
ELVERDINGHE.	11 Feb		Company marched from Watou to new camp behind ELVERDINGHE except 3 & 4 sections which entrained at Poperinghe for YPRES & marched thence to the Canal Bank one mile East of BRIELEN where they live in dugouts made by the 61st Co. The 60th Coy went into the trenches in front of canal	
	12th Feb		attack by Germans & heavy bombardment no work possible	
	13th Feb		Took reconnaissance of C.T.'s Canal to C.T.'s front line & Section Officers to front line & showed their work to men. Deep mud between F25-24 and no communication trench up to the front on the right. Pared C.T. in centre Celine Valley & Skipton road. Good bathing hut not much cover. A C.T. on the canal bank to the left but no C.T. trenches up to the front line on left. One section under 2nd Woodford known to improve & clean out the trench by cutting revetments extreme left. The gangway between F25-24 was made by No 3 section & SKIPTON ROAD was improved in several places. But no sound scheme of defence or means of tackling the enormous amount of work necessary to place this line in a good condition was decided on by the Brigade. I suggest that front line must be strongly held	
	14th Feb			

WAR DIARY
or
INTELLIGENCE SUMMARY

Army Form C. 2118.

83 Co RE

Place	Date	Hour	Summary of Events and Information	Remarks and references to Appendices
ELVERDINGHE	16-18 Feb.		Major Hopkins acted as CRE 2nd Divn & Capt Telfer commanded Company. Work was done on C.T. trenches & front line, but owing to want of settled programme of leading into the limited state of the lines so long, amount of work was under taken. Wynter Lane was improved & work was much hindered by Mg fire where kept direction & firing apt to them trecho in mind. In peril & front Capt Scott recommoters 731 which we weren't holding & found then a good bit of work. Fire trench was captured by the Germans & 733 recommoted & 730 also during the night through the latter was not attacked. Two gunners fell back on the Cavalry, Wynte lane & an attempt was made to bomb from the latter, & clear out Itchen was wounded with the bomb, & Lt Greenfield & supper Kellogn left. Rutman & some infantry wounded by shrapnel. Work was continued. Connecting up the recoveries into a first trench.	
	20 Feb.		Major Hopkins recommoted the ground for a new front line about 100yds behind the Evacuated line & found it so much shelled pitted as to be impracticable. Whilom Recovering & a post in target was continued.	
	21st Feb.		CRE recommoted a line still further back about 250yds forward RE & others decides to ...... this line	

Minshumont
Major RE 83 Co

Army Form C. 2118.

WAR DIARY
or
INTELLIGENCE SUMMARY
(Erase heading not required.)

2nd 83rd A.F.

Place	Date	Hour	Summary of Events and Information	Remarks and references to Appendices

ELVERDINGHE

22 Feb.
23 "
Wiring new line bays buy was done. Lines of ccremparts supplies. Headcover with trenchboard between.

4,83 P.6 A.E.

24.
83 AE
Parties on wiring hyper lane + improving wellpit deepened by Aug + Shrapnel fire. Somewhere on traffic trench knelled to target + on Rectounland

25.
Parties again sent out to wire hyperlane + half line completed. Wellpit newly again deepened by fire. Hyperborean sent at 2 a.m. to mend the whole front line + wire at night – heavy putt. now. – hyperlane wiring completed by 2 a.m. - bayonet when met a German patrol. Bayonet his wire during the night wiring hyperlane. + carrying scenario. Neg returns returned again afterwards & threw bombs with new work.

26.
Hyperlane wiring improvedly. Bayonet – Company relieved by B.W.C. + Major Stephen - Capt Tapp left the pigents for the canal for H.Q. near Boondeghe. M M McKennets

Army Form C. 2118.

83 Fullerphs

WAR DIARY
or
INTELLIGENCE SUMMARY.
(Erase heading not required.)

Place	Date	Hour	Summary of Events and Information	Remarks and references to Appendices
ELVERDINGHE	23rd		6th month period yesterday + Lt Hansl today. Smith & Baynes remain in dugouts in the canal to look after various. They report damage repaired to two bridges today	
	24th		Instructed by C.R.E II Army Army to relieve Fusiliers not many men on work.	

Murphy
Major
83 Co RE

83 JERE
vol 9

WAR DIARY or INTELLIGENCE SUMMARY

Army Form C. 2118.

83rd Ind. Co. R.E. (35)

Place	Date	Hour	Summary of Events and Information	Remarks and references to Appendices
ELVERDINGHE	4/3/16		Work on repairing bridges over the canal which are daily shelled & damaged. A new wooden bridge put in hand, trestles submerged & road very badly placed in position when required. R.E. O.P.S. improved & work done on R.E. workshop. Known way.	
	5/3/16		St Bayrold further demolished bridge 72 into Sk No gunrehn. Craters are demolished with difficulty. trying to rise of flood in Canal fraped lowland bridge is submerged. No excitem dugout in Canal bank (steel beard cover with 4 to 5ft sods & bowling bricks & concrete flows) had a direct hit by a 5.9 H.E. which did no damage beyond a bulge in the steel cover. Another French cover dugout which had been set to work at the bottom & contented on top collapsed & killed 3 men inside. Weather colder & wet.	
	6/3/16			
	7/3/16		Sleepers & rails continuing being reduced from Ypres & at the Potijze line to the junction with Wieltje.de Tramway. Subaltern were dropped within three c from Ypres. Heavy turn-fall hindered this & Cultivate can not till 9am could 4 un known by try to ground. Machine counts by rail get through in good time.	
	8/3/16			

Army Form C. 2118.

WAR DIARY
or
INTELLIGENCE SUMMARY
(Erase heading not required.)

83 Field Co RE

Place	Date	Hour	Summary of Events and Information	Remarks and references to Appendices
ELVERDINGHE	9/3/16		Six reinforcements joined –	
	10/3/16		N°4 section relieved N°2 section in canal bank. Enemy yesterday being inactive & having 48 hours rest takes a few rather sharp artillery strafes. Frontementiers have dead and much damage to Pioneers new trenches in half & west bank of canal at junction with French lines. Sent wagon loads of material supplement to Belmont Farm & Canal Bank for various works.	
	12.3.16. to 17.3.16		Completed two new bridges overcanal with approaches and a raft carrying pontoon somewhere to other bridge damaged by shellfire – completed a number of new dugouts – The corrugated steel trench cover carefully erected into the strongest cover & brick artwork tunnels has withstood several direct hits of 5-9 in shells. The tramway up to the canal has been very badly laid & reconstruction is delayed for lack of material. The work of revelling the trenches on the west canal bank much hindered by shellfire	

March 18th OC 83rd 7 Co R E

Army Form C. 2118.

(37)

WAR DIARY

INTELLIGENCE SUMMARY.

(Erase heading not required.)

Instructions regarding War Diaries and Intelligence Summaries are contained in F. S. Regs., Part II. and the Staff Manual respectively. Title pages will be prepared in manuscript.

8 3 ʳᵈ Field Co R.E.

Place	Date	Hour	Summary of Events and Information	Remarks and references to Appendices
ELVEDINGHE	18/3/16		Approach to 6 C bridge completed.	
	18.3.16 to 26.3.16		Work done repairing bridges + replacing old Dugouts by new ones also Tunnel Dugout proceeded with. Approaches to 6Y + 6X progressing. The work of revetting trenches on West Bank much hindered by trench mortar + aerial torpedo fire. From 7Y to 7Z completed over but a big gap blown in the middle which will not be revetted again. This gap cleared + trench boarded. From 7Z to Junction with French practically complete. Defences of two ends of West bank commenced, wiring completed from Junction with French to BOESINGHE Rd + pre-laying of look out post + loophole traverses commenced. Wiring in X Line continued also M.G.E. on X Line started. On 25/3/16 the M.G.E. by 7Z was blown in by a trench mortar bout is to be repaired. Reconstruction + repair of tramways in hand also Extension to the BRIELEN Rd	

M. a. H. C. S. N
Capt R.E.
27ᵗʰ March 1916
for O.C. 83ʳᵈ Co. R.E.

Army Form C. 2118.

WAR DIARY
or
INTELLIGENCE SUMMARY.

9th Suffolk Regt (38)

(Erase heading not required.)

Place	Date	Hour	Summary of Events and Information	Remarks and references to Appendices
ELVERDINGHE	27.3			
	28.3			
	29.3		Major Stephens returned from 7 days leave, hampered delays en route (by the Hospital). Pioneers wire into & out in front 30 men from our tank & pontoon work in front of Canal.	
	31.3		Capt. Cast went to command Bn to infancy. Hostile 6" shell & sh. shrap. from D4 to front line trenches. Major Stephens went to Brigade H.Qrs in the Canal. Fine weather & not much shelling. Germans began shelling our by-pass near 83 Co Camp.	
	April 1			

Murphy Mayor
O.C. 9 Suffolks

83 F C R E
Army Form C. 2118.
Vol 10

WAR DIARY
INTELLIGENCE SUMMARY.
(Erase heading not required.)

Place	Date	Hour	Summary of Events and Information	Remarks and references to Appendices
EVERDINGHE	April 1st		2 sections & 20 Miners proton relieving the Windsor Castle line to the Brielen Road.	
			Y. section relaying the rails between the railway & the Canal.	
	2 & 3		Shelling of trestle over canal much less than previously & unsuccessful.	
	4		New portion of 2O.R.A. came and the Company attached two for work. These officers were shown much work holes at the Canal bunks & land & water tramway.	
	5		Many new steel dugouts inhand on canal bank for the Infantry.	
	6		Put a maintenance gang of 1 Lieut & 15 men on the bivouacs & lines in dugouts on the Brielen Road & work on mornings & evenings at dusk.	
	7		2.O.R. banged by shrapnel fire. Work on tramway from BRIELEN Road to Canal bank carried on. No work done on X lines owing work on approaches to bridges 6x and 6D and on dugouts about which would be continued.	
	8		2/Lt HANDS went to hospital with throat trouble. Work as yesterday; with an X line being renewed. Rivers at 72: sandbagged up at a fire bay and worked on clearing the communication trench.	
	9		Pump taken up b.22 and water pumped out of H.Q.E. Rivers continued sandbags at C.T. and making a bombing straight.	R.A.D huttement 2 officers in of 85 75 type hr of

Army Form C. 2118.

WAR DIARY
or
INTELLIGENCE SUMMARY.
(Erase heading not required.)

Place	Date	Hour	Summary of Events and Information	Remarks and references to Appendices
ELVERDINGHE	10		Work on tramway carried on. Work on reclaiming a trench in rear x line continued in front of x line continued. Works on 72 and canal house as before. Weather has been fine and clear. Conditions for work out are excellent.	
	11		New bombing straight on 72 completed. Access to fire bay improved. ROTHERHAM ROAD destroyed by T.M's. Listening post near ridge completed. The Germans attacked opposite E27 in the evening, after a very heavy bombardment. They were repulsed.	
	12		No work on tramway and 72 done last night owing to enemy fire.	
	13		Tramway line linked up from BRIELEN road to Canal bank. Other works continued. Hospital coming bridge G.W. finished. Two bays of bridge 6 B. were laid in Steenflue and repaired. 1. O.R. reinforcement joined.	
	14		Work on packing tramline and putting in siding continued. M.G. C in railway embankment started. Loopholes covering bridges 4, 5, 6.3. completed. 2/Lt BAGNOLD returned from leave after six days extension on medical grounds. 2/Lt CHAMBERLAIN and advanced party from 2nd/2nd W.R. 7th Coy arrived to take over works.	R.Q.D. Water pipeline extension for ex. p.w.

WAR DIARY
or
INTELLIGENCE SUMMARY

Army Form C. 2118.

(Erase heading not required.)

Place	Date	Hour	Summary of Events and Information	Remarks and references to Appendices
ELVERDINGHE	15		Advanced party went to WINNEZEELE to arrange billets for the Company. 2/Lt CHAMBERLAIN shown over all works. Bridge 6.2 shelled and approach on WEST end blown in and repaired. For last few days the days have been wet and windy but the nights fine. No 3 section went up to Swing Bridge to take over work of 84th R.E. for this down. C. & "E" parade in morning, fatigues in afternoon. 4 men completed entrance to M.G.E. in railway embankment during the night. Weather fine in the morning and aircraft were active. Evening and night wet. 2 sections from 2/2nd W.R. Regt. under Lt BARLOW arrived	
	16.			
	17 F		3 sections returned to Kemmler at A18 d.80 by 10 pm after handing over to 17th 7th L. & N. Retiring P.o.C.	
	18 S		Company marched to Winnezeele. Tents not erected.	
	19 S.		Sections formed tents & made minor camp conveniences.	
	20 M.		Drill parade.	
	21 St } 22 nd }		Morning smoke helmet work for instruction of RAMC Personnel (20th Bath.). Plan of breakwater of Infantry Officers.	
	23 rd }		28th Sunday. Church parade.	
	24 F }		20 RE had two conference water service instruction, making complete water truck army report, etc.	
	25 F }		2nd Lt Bennett & advanced party left for Calais, morning of 25th. Weather fine & warm & leaves of trees coming out.	

WAR DIARY
or
INTELLIGENCE SUMMARY

Army Form C. 2118.

Place	Date	Hour	Summary of Events and Information	Remarks and references to Appendices
WINNEZEELE	26th		Company marched to Railway Siding Hopoutre arriving 12.45 a.m. Nov 29th. Line taken to entrain our railway trucks. Arrived Calais 8 a.m. Detrainment completed 10 a.m. Arrived No. 6 Rest Camp 12.30 p.m.	
Calais	27th			
"	28th		Took H.W. Gorton on board for repatriation. Company resting in camp. Men physically examined and refitted with warm clothing.	
"	29th		Lectures as per C.R.E's programme of training. Section water Section NCO's under instruction. Officer preparing return as ordered. Weather fine.	
"	30th		Company attends Climate parade. Weather fine.	

Elliots / RE
M.O.C. 65th Field Coy RE

B.M. 84.S.

Secret

83rd F^d Coy. R.E.

Ref. op. order 92
para (3) line 2
Delete the words "place
two sections" and substitute
the word "be".

24/4/16   A Hunt Maj
         B^{de} Maj 60 B^{de}

"C" Form (Duplicate).   Army Form C. 2123.
            MESSAGES AND SIGNALS.   No. of Message

                                    Charges to Pay.   Office Stamp.
                                    £   s.   d.

Service Instructions.

Handed in at _____ Office _____ m. Received _____ m.

TO   83rd FIELD COY R.E

Sender's Number	Day of Month	In reply to Number	AAA
7188	23/4/16		
One	long		out
			6 pm
convoy to	left	blankets to
station	AAA	long	not
be	delay		

FROM
PLACE & TIME   Coy R.E
                7.40 pm

O.C. 83rd Fd Coy R.E.
84
96

Maps.

In the event of the Division, while in
G.H.Q. Reserve, being ordered to
move to a locality outside the
2nd Army area, Brigades will collect
at once the following maps addressing
them to "2nd Army Maps", the no of unit
+ Division returning them being
clearly marked on the packages.
They will then be dumped at H.Qrs
occupied by the Brigade at the
time the move is ordered.
The issue of maps of the area to which
the Division is to proceed will
be carried out as soon as they
are received at Divnl H.Qrs.
Maps to be handed in: Sheets 27. 28
1/40,000; 27.N.W 28 NE, 27 NE
1/20,000. All trench maps. Sheet 13
CALAIS - DUNKIRK Sheet 14 any.

28/16

Captain R.E.
ADJUTANT R.E. 20th DIVISION

3   S.G. 841/60 B.

83rd Field Coy. R.E.

The position you select is not approved, it not being near enough to M & N camps and also the WATOU-POPERINGHE road will be carrying a lot of traffic & must not be blocked in any way.

The Brigadier directs that your position shall be on the POPERINGHE-DUNQUERQUE road immediately south of Bde H.Q. at 7.21.C.87.9.

24/4/16

A.C. Hunt Maj
Bde Maj 60 Bde.

Secret   B.M. 81. S

     83rd F. Coy. R.E.

Ref. O.O. 92 para (3)
Report immediately position
selected near Campe N & N.
Why has this not been done
already.

23/4/16   A. Lewis Maj.
         B de Maj, 60 B de

60th Brigade

83 Co position will be at Farms
at L2633 + 726 d31. Sheet 27
Delay regretted, the orders were
understood to be provisional
with move later place

Ap 24th 3hr   M. Maxwell
         OC 83 F Co

To. O.C. 83rd Field Coy R.E.

The following is a suitable route from WATOU to F.21.

E.28.d – E.29.b
Thence turn SOUTH and take the first turning EAST to F.25.a

OR. E.29.b – E.30.a and then turn SOUTH on to the same road as above.

The Northern of the two alternative routes from E.30.a to F.25.a is quite impracticable as the road is unmetalled.

Then F.25.a – F.21.a thence turn SOUTH along the DUNKERQUE–POPERINGHE road to F.22.d.o.6

The road is about 5 metres wide between ditches. Only the centre 2 metres are metalled. Two columns can pass if one halts.

The road is in a poor state the whole way and would be awkward if the march had to be made by night.

A good site for a bivouac is the avenue running EAST from the POPERINGHE-DUNKERQUE road at F.22.d.0.6.
It is about 7 metres between the inner rows of trees, and there are two outer rows about 6 metres outside these.
Officers could be billeted either in the Estaminet on the North side of the road just opposite the avenue, or at the house at the E. end of av.
There is a well and water tank handy for the water supply.
There were no very suitable billets for the company in the immediate vicinity.

R.A.D. Water
Lieut RE

25.4.16.

OC 83rd Field Coy R.E.
~~E4~~
~~96~~
~~20th Signal Coy R.E.~~

SECRET

20th Divn Defence Scheme while in
                    Corps Reserve.
In the event of movement being
ordered and the Division being
concentrated in the area.
   WATOU — PROVEN — POPERINGE (exclusive).

1. BAGGAGE. All units before
marching off will pack their
baggage waggons & have them
at their present headquarters
(except the Bde at CALAIS). They
will be collected under orders
of O.C. Divnl Train and be
parked at WINNEZEELE (off the road)

2. No second line transport will
accompany units

3. The supply sections of the train
will be collected under the orders
of the O.C. Divnl Train and will park
off the road at DROGLANDT, whence
they will return after refilling

4. Refilling Point WATOU.

21 7/16   H. Mause.

SECRET. Copy No 3.

19.4.16.

20th Divn Operation Order No 54

Movements of Brigades.

1. The 61st Bde group will march from CALAIS on 26th April & arrive WORMHOUDT area on 28th April.

   The 60th Bde Group will rail from Camps area to CALAIS commencing on 26th April & completing on 27th April.

   The 59th Bde Group will march on 26th & 27th April from WORMHOUDT area to Camps area and replace the 60th Inf. Bde. Group unit for unit as soon as the camps or billets are vacated by 60th Bde.

2. The 60th Bde Group will march from CALAIS on 6th May & arrive WORMHOUDT area on 8th May.

   The 59th Bde Group will rail from Camps area to CALAIS commencing on 6th May & completing on 7th May.

   The 61st Bde

2 (Cont'd.) The 61st Bde Group will march on 6th & 7th May from WORMHOUDT area to Camps area & replace the 59th Inf. Bde Group unit for unit as soon as the camps or billets are vacated by the 59th Bde Group.

3. Units of the Brigade group in camps area will entrain for CALAIS in the following order:-

1 Battalion	1st Train.
Brigade H.Q.	
Signals	} 2nd Train.
Machine Gun Coy	
1 Battalion	3rd Train.
A.S.C. & Fd. Ambulance	4th Train.
Field Co. R.E.	5th Train.
1 Battalion	6th Train.
1 Battalion	7th Train.

Rail Time Tables will be issued later.

4. Should the Reserve Bus be required after departure of the 2nd Train the G.O.C. WORMHOUDT Brigade area will assume

4. (cont'd)

command of the troops remaining in the Camps area.

5. Acknowledge.

      Sgd. W. Madocks
              Lieut. Col
    G.S. 20th Divn.

Vol 11

WAR DIARY or **INTELLIGENCE SUMMARY**
Army Form C. 2118.

83rd Field Coy RE

Place	Date	Hour	Summary of Events and Information	Remarks and references to Appendices
Calais	May 1st 1916		Sections engaged in carrying out technical schemes in accordance with programme drawn up by C.R.E. 2nd Division. Weather fine.	
	May 2nd 1916		Sections schemes continued as yesterday. Weather fine. Thunderstorm & heavy rain storm afternoon.	
	May 3rd 1916		Sections schemes continued as yesterday. Weather fine very hot.	
	May 4th 1916		No 3 section complete returns. No 2 Section repairs duck and rifle screens.	
	May 5th 1916		No 1 & No 4 section on pontoon practice (using trestles) weather fine very hot. 11/Fd Amb'ce RAP originally through River Boating. Rennell to casino (hospital). Adrian party under 11/Fd went proceeded to Wizernes. Section engaged with repair duck and rifle screens.	
	May 6		March to ZUTKERQUE.	
	May 7		March to VOLKERINGHOVE	
	May 8		Co. arrived at Ledringhem 2mls S of ESQUELBEC. hytroppeme repaired Company. Weather showery.	
	May 9		At Ledringhem remain all day leads at 9 PM orders of movement given.	

Army Form C. 2118.

WAR DIARY
or
INTELLIGENCE SUMMARY.
(Erase heading not required.)

63 Field Co.

Instructions regarding War Diaries and Intelligence Summaries are contained in F. S. Regs., Part II. and the Staff Manual respectively. Title pages will be prepared in manuscript.

Place	Date	Hour	Summary of Events and Information	Remarks and references to Appendices
LEDRINGHEM	May 10	—	Pontoon drill + gas helmet drill. Fine weather.	
	May 11		1+4 sections left for BRIELEN by Bus. Relieves 84th Co. working on 2nd Line defences there. Remainder pontooning + gas helmet drill	
	May 12		Drill + making up concertina barbed wire obstacles. 2/Capt West-Partrick posted as 2nd Capt. Sapper Talbot-Graham made Lance Corpl.	
	May 13		Raining — Making up wire concertinas + drilling. Worked at Winnezeele. Cpl Hyatt, Sgt Grew, Shaw, McDonald went on leave to England.	
	May 14		Major Hopkins took defences class at Winnezeele. 9.30 to 12/30 pm	
	May 15		Sections working up concertina wire — Major Hopkins ran to Winnezeele for infantry class	
	May 16		Drill + instruction in demolition of bridges.	
WINNEZEELE	May 17		Company moved to Winnezeele and 1+4 sections returned to Winnezeele. Major Hopkins & Capt West & Partrick joined 76th Co. at VLAMERTINGHE to take over new line. Major Hopkins	
	May 18		went into YPRES + see Co. 76th Co. Major Hopkins went up to YPRES + went round the trenches with Co 76th Co.	
VLAMERTINGHE	May 19		Company marched to VLAMERTINGHE. Fine + hot since May 15th.	

W.M. Hopkins
Major R.E.
O.C. 83 Field Co. R.E.

Army Form C. 2118.

WAR DIARY
or
INTELLIGENCE SUMMARY.
(Erase heading not required.)

83 Field Coy RE

Instructions regarding War Diaries and Intelligence Summaries are contained in F. S. Regs., Part II. and the Staff Manual respectively. Title pages will be prepared in manuscript.

Place	Date	Hour	Summary of Events and Information	Remarks and references to Appendices
YPRES	May 20th		Section marched to Cellars in YPRES & took over from 75th Co.	
	21st		60 Brigade relieved the 2nd Guards Brigade, with area roughly on either side of the YPRES ROULERS railway and 83 Co. operated with them.	
	22nd		Sections working in front line with 60 Brigade	
	23rd		Works in hand: 3. Concrete M.G.E - new in front of Hotel Chateau. Improvements to KROMBEEN	
	24th F			redoubt outside
	25th S		Weather turned wet.	Ramparts of YPRES.
	26th M		Rain at night, breaking between improvements of culverts & junction of infantry comns
	27th T		the railway. Espex Hazards wounded by shell in MENIN Road on 28th May
			Looking up of M.G.E. & dugouts	
			2d bayonet exchange of scheme for counterattacking defences of Canton near Railway wood
			& started with 150mm. dugsny necessary trenches	
	28th		Capt Greville wounded by shell fire in YPRES.	
	29th			
	30th		arranged to blow up wire front German trench now heading wood but delayed	
	31st		by infantry & has to fort front it	

M[signature]
[signature]
Capt RE
OC 83 Fld Co

CBS/40

D.A.G.
3rd Echelon

Herewith War Diary of
83rd Field Co R.E. for the
period 1st to 30th June 1916.

30/6/16

E. White Lieut R.E.
for O.C. 83rd Fd Co R.E.

WAR DIARY
INTELLIGENCE SUMMARY
(Erase heading not required.)

Army Form C. 2118

Place	Date	Hour	Summary of Events and Information	Remarks and references to appendices
YPRES	1.6.16		Btr trained & Coperatives & Welcom put out two Explodes into the German wire (one) captured at I.12.a.31 but enemy parties infantry was driven in before Explodes were exploded. Torpedoes were not recovered but Exploder brought in from between lines. German attack on Sanctuary wood and company standing to.	
"	2.6.16			
"	3.6.16		New C.T. approaching Railwaywood reconnd 15ogs. New events M.G.E. in Railway bank near Hellfire corner reconnd. Dugs new fire trench 200y's long south side of muddy lane and cleaned out old C.T. from Railway Dump to P.S. Muddylane between West lane	
5	4.6.16			
	5.6.16			
	6.6.16		Cut out new Reserve line trench	
			Cuts between & drainage.	
	7.6.		strand & bridges. Enemy begun a new trench to connect into Canadian newerypt trench being trench starting at 4.6. but found it an impossible situation being overlooked by Germans trench Fry & noted a support trench behind it 15 & 17. June 8	

Army Form C. 2118.

WAR DIARY
of
INTELLIGENCE SUMMARY.
(Erase heading not required.)

83rd Qs C R E

Place	Date	Hour	Summary of Events and Information	Remarks and references to Appendices
YPRES	8/6/16		Started putting in gun emplacements in H.16 & H.20 but secured very difficult & little done.	
	9/6.		Continued work on emplacements by day & got three done.	
	10/6.		Cameron all day emplacements. Using 30 Pioneers + 20 Sappers + 80 emplacement soft by completed by 10 p.m.	
	11/6		Completed emplacements. Weather very wet.	
	12/6		Finish garrison work. Carporals started new Sapper Burns & Pres. Prep. arose changes for demolition of enemy's new dept. arose about 10.15 p.m. & the new arrangements. Gun was put off at 11.30 a.m. & new rendezvous near Tuesday. Weather warmer, rain later.	
	13/6		Work continued on M.G. emplacements.	
	14/6		Work in progress drawing Duck walk.	
	15/6		Drain dug to Duck walk. Work continued on M.G. emplacements. Weather still wet. Work walk drainage continued, also drainage to hind trench water running away well. Heavy trench storm heavy damages during the day. Work on M.G. emplacements continues.	

E.W.White Lt Col

WAR DIARY
or
INTELLIGENCE SUMMARY.

Army Form C. 2118.

83 25 CRL

Place	Date	Hour	Summary of Events and Information	Remarks and references to Appendices
Y Camp	16/6		Work on M.G. emplacements continued. Men took over new Frontage 11 wire entanglements at 4 p.m. by "A" & "B" gunteams in conjunction with Brigade orders. Practically no work was done by teams of men. Work being done to K.70 portion did not materialize until 4.30 a.m. in view of three draughts and draught moonlight.	
Y Camp	17/6		The Souter Salt Cat Portage reference was now signpost reference employed from Frontage to Bide Short. Brick work entirely cleaned out dragout wiring Battalion Items Arrests out. A quiet night & fine.	
"	19/6		Work on entanglements continued. Repairs to M.G. & M.G.11. completed except repairs were carried on at Duke Street on battleship trenches. Two work on continuous was to continue dump by charge of campany. Spare emplacements further cleared out & puttied . Now to begin bombers up with trenches. Bombers stood for in the parade ground to distance of 60 yards. Much noise probably result of wind.	
	20/6		Salt in full was completed to waist to work on M.O.E's continued. Heavy trench dragout & Parapet were deeper Also Just put a distance of 50 yards. Trench 9/15 drained & Parapet raised 2 feet.	
			20/6/18	

Army Form C. 2118.

WAR DIARY
or
INTELLIGENCE SUMMARY.
(Erase heading not required.)

83 Tunnel Co. R.E.

Instructions regarding War Diaries and Intelligence Summaries are contained in F.S. Regs., Part II. and the Staff Manual respectively. Title pages will be prepared in manuscript.

Place	Date	Hour	Summary of Events and Information	Remarks and references to Appendices
YPRES	20/6		For 100 yards trophies into G.E. Railway farm tunnels. Work in M.G.E's continues. Weather fine.	
	21/6		B.C. M.G. dugout completed. Muddy tram deepened two feet 100 yards forward. Junction S.1.B. Work proceeding powerful & dummy. Work in M.G.E's continues. M.G. emplacement outpost farm repaired. Not completed. Work in M.G.E's continues. Weather fine.	
	21–27/6		Work on M.G.E. continued. Work progress on muddy tram & S.18. Work on reservoir & drainage. Work with hinds continued. Weather fine.	
	27/28/6		Work on M.G.E. continues. Work on muddy tram, S.18 and breakwork also weld in reservoir. Weather fine. Sergt Richards wounded in Muddyland.	
	24/6		Major Hopkins (now Capt.) struck to Warrington. New tunnel at Torr marked out.	
	25.6.		Raid by left brigade with somewhat headed by shelling.	
	26.6.			
	27.6		Emergency shelters being carried to front line and not much work possible except on M.G.E's in reserves.	
	28.6			
	29.6		Raid by right Brigade. 2nd Lt Jackson & Sergt Mackey both wounded with German Tunnels into explosives & dating knives but none were found.	
	30.6		Major Stephens succeeded as O.C. School in Consolidation of trenches. Weather fine.	

W Stephens
Major

20th Divisional Engineers.

83rd FIELD COMPANY R. E.

JULY 1916

July

Army Form C. 2118.

WAR DIARY
or
INTELLIGENCE SUMMARY.
(Erase heading not required.)

83 Field Coy RE

Vol 13

Instructions regarding War Diaries and Intelligence Summaries are contained in F.S. Regs., Part II. and the Staff Manual respectively. Title pages will be prepared in manuscript.

Forwarded Mallard
Col. C.R.E. 20th Divn.

Place	Date	Hour	Summary of Events and Information	Remarks and references to Appendices
YPRES	1/7/16		Major J.A. Shields + Sprox [Gittermond?] to [meet?]. Brigadier General [Inito?] + Major Hopkins found ret-spen M.G.E. near Outpost Farm and inspected other works.	
	2/7/16		Sapper Archer [bad?], [wounded?] by [machinegun?] in billet in YPRES. Sapper Mills killed by [shell?] on Menin Road. Kept buffers [fully?] occupied. [removing?] Saw [cylinder?] stakes at allocated labour.	
	3/7/16		Fired site of 3 M.G.E. near C.16 letter into M.G.O.	
	4/7/16		Two selected dugouts have [blasted?] to [enlarge?] myself. Aeroplane attached	See APP. No 1.
	5/7.		2nd M.G.E. near 70 into M.G.O.	
	6/7.		[Staved?] 1 M.G.E. [drawing?] attached	See APP. No 2.
	7/7.		Rainy weather Continues. No German shell fire or snipers but our batteries fire from now on.	
	8/7		[Average?] number of [sapers?] working inside RE 350, with 250 more working independently or for C.R.E. or Town Major YPRES.	
	9/7.		[In-French?] on night [much?] enforced by [Pioneers?] and inch [strong?] than night [previously?]. Site for M.G.E. near [Posonlij?] passed by Major [Hopkins?]	

July 11 W[?] [signed]

Army Form C. 2118.

WAR DIARY
or
INTELLIGENCE SUMMARY

(Erase heading not required).

83 Field A. R.S.

Instructions regarding War Diaries and Intelligence Summaries are contained in F.S. Regs., Part II. and the Staff Manual respectively. Title pages will be prepared in manuscript.

Place	Date	Hour	Summary of Events and Information	Remarks and references to Appendices
YPRES	10.7		People on left convoy and in which reported repeated arrivals & 20 R.S. work was attempted out of YPRES.	
	11.7		Bombardment, work continued on new trench & M.S.T.S. by order orders	SEE APP. 5
	12.7		Report intercallation of St Jacques Church attached	
	13.7		Work continued on trenches & M.S.T.S. Capt Matt wounded whilst going to help wounded man near the Cathedral	
	14.7		Gilbert & Hyland wounded whilst men from made heavy shelling of Cathedral	
	15.7		Work continued in trenches L.M. G. F.S.	
VLAMERTINGHE	16.7		Rendezvous work in Trenches & Boston Fields. and moved front pictures back to Menin Trench.	
HOUTKERQUE	17.7		Bivouacked moved by train to Houthorpe and transport beyond	
	18.7		Resting	
BERTHEN	19.7		Marched to BERTHEN at 3pm. arrived here 7pm. artillery march	

1577 Wt. W.10791/1773 500,000 1/15 D.D. & L. A.D.S.S./Forms/C. 2118.

WAR DIARY
INTELLIGENCE SUMMARY

Army Form C. 2118.

83 Field Co RE

Place	Date	Hour	Summary of Events and Information	Remarks and references to Appendices
METTE EGLISE	20.7		Marched to Neuvilles + Bernard. Took over some maps from Coy C + handed one off. Post lies at Northuman. [illegible] H.Qrs + parts at 101 Co H.Qr. Fine + warm.	
HANOVRE	21.7		Marched to Brononchi. Took over billets + shops of 103 Co + CRE's dumps. There at HQ CRE took about 100 turbines + workshops. Officers visits units of 104 Co, 103 Co + 105 Co + Maj Hopkins took relay allusion from OC 103 Co + 104 Co + Saw OC Northumbrian DC about other works which was already been handed over to him by the 104 + 103 Cos.	
St Jan Cappel	22.7		Marched to Jan Cappel at 11am. Orders received to march at 9.15 am + to hand over billets + works to 7th ? Co. Spoke to OC 7th Co on telephone + Lt J.H. Jackson to hand over. OC 7th Co refused to take over as he said he had no orders to do so. 2nd ? Preliminary company + left HQ in charge of books + kept. Maj Hopkins reports GHQs 8 + 10pm in afternoon + received instructions to withdraw the latter of no officer could take them over before the Company marched.	

M.M. [signature]
OC 83rd Co. RE

Army Form C. 2118.

WAR DIARY
or
INTELLIGENCE SUMMARY.
(Erase heading not required.)

83rd Field Co. R.E.

Place	Date	Hour	Summary of Events and Information	Remarks and references to Appendices
	23.7		Halted at St Jans Cappel.	
	24.7		Marched at 2pm to HOUDEGHEM	
	25.7		Marched to BAVINCHOVE at 5pm and entrained at 7pm in 1 hour 30 min. Left at 9.57 pm.	
	26.7		Detrained at DOULLENS and marched to LUCHEUX arriving 8am went into billets and marched again at 4/40 pm and bivouaced at SARTON with Tea Brigade. Weather had been hot.	
	27.7		Marched to VAUCHELLES at 4pm & bivouaced here. Major Hopkins & Lt Baynolds Jackson went to COURCELLES & 151 SCRE to take over work.	
	28.7		9/151st Co. & Capt White marched Company to Courcelles sending 3 sections to COLINCAMPS & Hemencourt & the D.S.T.L with transport at Rossignol Farm.	
	29.7		Working on French Mining Sups & Shafts, Meyrin site & dugouts & maintaining water supply Trench to 929. Major Hopkins visited COLINCAMPS - Brigade H.Q Bn - Bn. T.M.O & CRE at GUIN.	
	30.7			

M. Hopkins
OC 83 Co 83 Field Co RE

20th Divisional Engineers.

83rd FIELD COMPANY R. E.

AUGUST 1 9 1 6

83rd Field Coy RE

SECRET

83 F E RE

VOL 14

Army Form C. 2118.

WAR DIARY
or
INTELLIGENCE SUMMARY.
(Erase heading not required.)

Place	Date	Hour	Summary of Events and Information	Remarks and references to Appendices
COURCELLES	31/7		Brichin interchgt WHITE busy in outposts at OSIN CH MES and working in front line on trench mortar emplacements. Kheips dugouts with artillery labour coyls. 2 lorries + 10 wagons fetching materials from B RE Parks and 4 RE wagons + 3 Rab wagons taking men rushing & new materials up to trenches at night. Fine & very hot.	Co-rds-Copt RE for the 83rd Fd Co RE
	1.8			
	2.8		Head Qrs of Company moved camp to Courcelles Village from "The Dell". 2 Heavy + 2 double medium Trench mortar emplacements at Minuet trench line intact. & two double Stokes dug dugouts. Major Hopkins went round trenches with 2 O.C. knights. Major Woodroffe till present for instruction on RE& L duties.	
	3.8			
	4.8			
	5.8			
	6.8		2 O.C. Major Woodroffe took over the trenches.	
	7.8		Advanced section moved camp from Co bivi camps to Courcelles to make room for 25 Divn. Forbrien Courcelles troops from 84th Co.	
	8.8		Work on T.M. emplacements and full in water bowsers and filled to return bowsers. From water points.	

Army Form C. 2118.

WAR DIARY
or
INTELLIGENCE SUMMARY.
(Erase heading not required.)

Instructions regarding War Diaries and Intelligence Summaries are contained in F. S. Regs., Part II. and the Staff Manual respectively. Title pages will be prepared in manuscript.

Place	Date	Hour	Summary of Events and Information	Remarks and references to Appendices
Bouzincourt	9	8/6	Save attachment 150 men of D.C.L.I. attached for working parties on T.M. Emplacements work on T.M. Emplacements & front line trenches and containers. Work continues during 15 minute enemy bombardment.	
Bouzincourt	10.		Work progresses on exteriors and gas proof. Major Hopkins inspected emplacements of company and provision. Major Brunswick arrived and took over command of new company. Work continued on T.M. emplacements etc.	
Bouzincourt	11.		O.C. & Capt. Woit went round and inspected work in progress. Work continues satisfactorily.	
Courcelles	12	day & night shifts continuous work	Work in progress: No 1 Sect: 1 heavy Trenchmortar Emplacement with tool store housed out 1 medium 1 deep dugout in front line 2 shafts and 8 dugouts 2 additional dugouts with tool store No 3 Sect: 1 H.T.M. Emplacement 2 a (tomato type) No 1 Sect: 1 deep dugout in progress with tanks from ? water supply 1 membrane for F.S.E. sandbagged for protection No 4 Sect: Trench stores at works shops in TOURCELLES.	15m actt infantry 8 actty
"	13		do . . . do . . . Night work delayed by account of expected raid.	

Ralph H. Sayer?
Lt. Col.
? 7 ? 16

Army Form C. 2118.

WAR DIARY
or
INTELLIGENCE SUMMARY.
(Erase heading not required.)

Instructions regarding War Diaries and Intelligence Summaries are contained in F. S. Regs., Part II. and the Staff Manual respectively. Title pages will be prepared in manuscript.

Place	Date	Hour	Summary of Events and Information	Remarks and references to Appendices
COURCELLES	Aug 14		Work attached on the railway. Night shifts much delayed by reconnection expected raid, and relief of Brigade	
"	15th		Brigade relief's again delayed anyhow, worked ceased at 12 noon handed over to 75th Pl Coy R.E. Brunghe dump	
	16th	9.30am	Coy marched off picking up motor lot section at COIGNEUX. marched via ST LEDGER — AUTHIE — THIEVRES to AMPLIER. westwards to HDQS about 12.30pm	
AMPLIER	17th		Coy rested	
AMPLIER	18th	5.00am	Coy marched off marched via DOULLENS — CANDAS — FIENVILLERS to ST HILAIRE where the Coy westwards bivouacs at about 12 noon.	
ST HILAIRE	19th	9 am	Transport Coy and all except one horses marched off under Capt White to NADURS where they were billeted for the night. Dismounted portion of Coy bivouacked at ST HILAIRE.	
ST HILAIRE	20th	7.30am	Having received no orders Dismounted portion of Coy backloaded via FIENVILLERS to CANDAS. Detrained bien entrained at CANDAS. travelled via CANDAS — CONDE — AMIENS to MERICOURT Station.	
		2 pm		
VILLE SUR ANCRE		7.45pm	Marched from MERICOURT to VILLE SUR ANCRE. When Coy marched from station on the marched portion of Coy joined up had with dismounted portion edge of the town.	
VILLEBRUNE	21st	9.30am	Coy marched off via MEAULTE to France 57.01 killage. arrive about 12 noon.	
MEAULTE	22nd	8 am	No. 3 Section marched off to BRAY for recruitment to R.E. dump.	
		2 pm	Coy marched off under Capt White to FRICOURT CANNOT where some further enlistments were arrive. Dismounted horses. Bivouacked Bivouac under Capt White	
CORNOY				

1577 Wt.W10791/1773 500,000 1/15 D.D.&L. A.D.S.S./Forms/C. 2118.

WAR DIARY
INTELLIGENCE SUMMARY

Army Form C. 2118.

Place	Date	Hour	Summary of Events and Information	Remarks and references to Appendices
CARNOY	Aug 23rd		Company in Reserve with 55th Bde. Took over dump from 24th Divn. and 14 men sent down to BRAY. Knocked at dump there.	
		6 p.m.	No 1 Section to Tramque to dig attack trenches in front line at GUILLEMONT. Owing to a German attack no work was possible instead of Rhilletts about 3 a.m.	
CARNOY	24th	4 a.m.	2nd Lt SMITH set out and 3000 yds of Cable Trench from THE CRATERS E of TRONES WOOD. Working party of 700 men. Trench completed at 2 p.m.	
"	25th	5 a.m.	Work done. LEINSTER ALLEY widened and deepened for 200 yds E of TRONES WOOD by No 3 Section by No 4 section. TRONES ALLEY went round the trenches	
	26th		Work done LEINSTER ALLEY continued. New new trench started from E sect. of TRONES WOOD. Advanced Brigade dumps started at west edge of TRONES WOOD CO & 2nd Lt BAGNOLD set out new trenches North of GUILLEMONT.	
	27th		Corduroy track started through BERNAFAY WOOD. Two lanes cut through TRONES WOOD Assembly Trench started behind TRONES WOOD. Outbreak of cholera elsewhere S.M. admitted to hospital.	
	28th		Tracks through BERNAFAY & TRONES WOODS improved. Advanced Bath HQ started argent opposite GUILLEMONT	

Ralph ... Lt Col
... 83rd ... RE
... Coy

Army Form C. 2118.

WAR DIARY
or
INTELLIGENCE SUMMARY.
(Erase heading not required.)

Place	Date	Hour	Summary of Events and Information	Remarks and references to Appendices
CARNOY.	29/9/16		Nos 1 & 4 sections prepared an attack position for the Company in DUMMY TRENCH. Company work through BERNAFAY WOOD. All nights work cancelled owing to bad weather.	
	30/9/16		The state of the roads & trenches very bad. Work almost impossible owing. Tracks continued through BERNAFAY WOOD to the run & the state of the trenches. Work cancelled by division	

[signature]
Lt RE
for OC 93rd Ft CoyRE

20th Divisional Engineers.

83rd FIELD COMPANY R. E.

SEPTEMBER 1 9 1 6

WAR DIARY or INTELLIGENCE SUMMARY

Army Form C. 2118.

83rd Field Coy. R.E.

Place	Date	Hour	Summary of Events and Information	Remarks and references to Appendices
Carnoy	31/8/16		No 3 & 4 Sections forming trolley track near Carnoy for work; working party work anticipated by him skilled. No 2 Section constructing dug-out for new Brunner construction party. No 1 Section constructing new Cornwall Alley & Sunwood Trench. Work anticipated with by Cottern and gas attacks arrived first.	
"	1/9/16		No 3 & 4 Section forming trolley near Carnoy. No 1 Section completing work also working party. No 2 Section completing dug-out for new Brunner construction party. Work anticipated as anticipated by gas attacks. Howitzer battery part of hospital was weather fine.	
"	2/9/16		No 2 Section & part No 4 Section cleaning & remaking trenches. No work done on two sections as this section is in support & work on new trench is depth is assistance operations.	
"	3/9/16		8.00pm completion of new battle position in Carnoy. Work in connection with O.C. 83rd Brunny started at 3.30am No 3 & No 4 sections carried on as details of arrangement with the work of assistance of gentlemen at 2.45pm. No 1 section was accurate work in bravery of trench T19C69 & T19C56. Assault trench T19C.18.	
"	4/9/16		Work on consolidation of gentlemen continuing by No 2.3.4 Sections. Shorts Posts T19C6 & which were also attended to group of 40 men which were evaluated trench were shortly about 35 which were consolidated.	
"	5/9/16		T19C6 & was completed at 1.55am & the remained men in front of them.	
"	6/9/16		Coy. formed at 1.45am & was evacuated at approx.	
Bray	7/9/16		Squad marched by march to Bray. Commenced new billets at 10pm	
Vaux	8/9/16 9/9/16		Coy. one march arrived in Vaux which required rest & considered necessary. Arrangements made with support for sanitation.	

WAR DIARY
or
INTELLIGENCE SUMMARY.
(Erase heading not required.)

Army Form C. 2118.

Place	Date	Hour	Summary of Events and Information	Remarks and references to Appendices
S.23.c.5.3 BERNAFAY WOOD	17.9.16	3 a.m.	O.C. and 2 officers and 2 N.C.O's reconnoitred front trenches held by 60th Bde. EAST of GINCHY.	MAP.M
		8 a.m.	Company moved forward to bivouac 300 x N of GUILLEMONT. Took over upper BERNAFAY WOOD.	
GUILLEMONT T.12.1.3		4 p.m.	3 Sections set about Nos. 1 & 4 digging assembly trench in T.9.d. behind front line with 50 D.L.I pioneers. T.9.b. 0.8. with 50 pioneers.	Sheet 57 C
			No.2 Sec. digging assembly trench in T.9.d. behind front line with 50 D.L.I pioneers.	DLI
			This and 3 Sections returned at different times.	form
GUILLEMONT	18.9.16	4 a.m.	3 Sections out	
		8 p.m.	No.2 Sec. Renewing Garman old behind trench in T.9.b.	
			No.3 — digging New trench Northern hew road T.9.a. 9.9. and T.3.c.	
			No.4 — With 4 Coy 17 D.L.I Sussex	
			Deepening and improving Trench S.93 – New road T.9.b.0.8	
BERNAFAY WOOD	19.9.16	6 a.m.	Sections returned to bivouac at BERNAFAY WOOD N/N.E. 2nd dug-out.	
		6.30 p.m.	No.1 Sec. with 50 D.L.I pioneers proceed to spin/continued trench S. of sunken road from about T.9.b. 2.7½ to T.9.b. 2.4.7½. Length about 400 yds depth 4'6".	
			No.3 Sec. improving trench No.9 sunken road T.9.a. 9.9. and T.3.c. and 10 exit strips made from it. depth 4'6"	
CITADELLE F.21.9.r.	20.9.16	7 a.m.	Sections returned to bivouac at CITADEL 4th Coy. E. Lanes wet weather which made work heavy and the difficulty getting up trench duty. trenches 12.18" deep in heavy mud was always unpleasant. Made a good deal of trouble on account	
		4 p.m.	No.2 Sec. paraded and went on work to BERNAFAY WOOD not party of 150 D.L.I. Work done Entrance of trench South of sunken road to assembly trench along C engaging 177/8m. N of T.9.b. 2.7. 4.7. to T.1.b. 4.2.0. distance about 925x. (ii) Joined up front about T.9.b. 4.3.0. front line T.9.b. 6.0. distance about 650x. Trenches all 4'6" deep and about 2' wide made on 7.9.7.9 with traverses.	
"	21.9.16	6.30	Section out all night return at 8 this a.m. Company loaded up horsedrawn wagons and rested.	

Jas. [Signature]
Capt. R.E.
O.C. 83 Rd Sd. Co R.E.

Army Form C. 2118.

WAR DIARY
or
INTELLIGENCE SUMMARY.
(Erase heading not required.)

Instructions regarding War Diaries and Intelligence Summaries are contained in F.S. Regs., Part II. and the Staff Manual respectively. Title pages will be prepared in manuscript.

Place	Date	Hour	Summary of Events and Information	Remarks and references to Appendices
VAUX sur SOMME	10/9/16		Inspection of Company by G.O.C. Company employed in turfing dugouts & forming up.	
"	11/9/16		Capt White was hospitalised with poisoned hand. Company paraded at 12.30 pm marched to billets at Méault' via a motor convoy arriving at 4.10 pm.	
Méault	12/9/16		120 men of the company had hot baths.	
"	13/9/16		100 men of the company had hot baths.	
"	14/9/16		Capt Pennefeather attended a conference of CRE's in the afternoon. "Fothergate" went forward to do its turfing. Company under Lt Behan marched from Méault at 4.30 pm and arrived at camp at F.21.9.5.7 at 6 pm. Men in tents & bivouacs.	
F.21.9.5.7 (Méault)	15/9/16		Company ready horses at 5 am notice. Moved off at 12.35 pm with horses & transport carts only, rest of transport thereafter reassumed under 1st Pld Regt. No stores carried.	
Bois de TALUS			Company moved to A.Q.C. Bois de Talus reached 1.30 pm. Rained commenced about 8 pm. very cold.	
BERNAFAY WOOD	16.9.16	5.30 am	Company marched off and bivouacked North of BERNAFAY WOOD S23 C 5.3.	

J.C. Pay Capt
Capt R.E.

Capt

WAR DIARY
INTELLIGENCE SUMMARY.

(Erase heading not required.)

Army Form C. 2118.

Instructions regarding War Diaries and Intelligence Summaries are contained in F.S. Regs., Part II. and the Staff Manual respectively. Title pages will be prepared in manuscript.

Place	Date	Hour	Summary of Events and Information	Remarks and references to Appendices
Reference Map	Sept.		ALBERT Combined Sheet 57D.S.E. 57C S.W. 62D N.E. 62C N.W. 40,000	
F21a8.4	22	12.30 p.m.	Company marched to billets at TREUX J6 a 7.3	
TREUX	23		Cleaned harness, wagons, equipment. Company bathed.	
"	24		Church parade	
"	25	4.30 p.m.	Marched to Citadel (F21 a 8.4) via VILLE-SUR-ANCRE and MORLANCOURT	
F21 a 8.4	26	9.0 a.m.	Marched via Cross Country tracks to S.E. (MALTZ HORN valley) to S.E. Corner of TRONES WOOD in bivouac. Transport at A4 b 8.0	
S30 c 0.7 TRONES WOOD.	27	9.30 a.m.	Transport moved to MARICOURT A16 a 9.1. Nos 1 & 3 Sections with Co. B 11th D.L.I. worked on road between GUILLEMONT and GINCHY in afternoon	
S30 C 0.7	28		12 men from each section went to LONGUEVAL in afternoon to prepare dug outs for Company's occupation.	
S30 C 0.7	29		Company in reserve. Two Sections went to LONGUEVAL to prepare dug outs.	
"	30th		Nos 1, 2 & 4 Sections making track North of GINCHY N.E. towards GUEDECOURT. No 3 Section clearing disposable dugouts in LONGUEVAL.	
LONGUEVAL.		3.30	Dismantled portion of Company marched to LONGUEVAL where lay billeted in dug outs and cellars	

Jas. Parry M.
Capt M.G.
O.C. 83rd Coy M.G. Corps

20th Divisional Engineers.

83rd FIELD COMPANY R. E.

OCTOBER 1 9 1 6

Vol 16

83rd Field Coy

WAR DIARY
or
INTELLIGENCE SUMMARY.
(Erase heading not required.)

Army Form C. 2118.

[Stamp: 83rd FIELD COMPANY R.E.]

Place	Date	Hour	Summary of Events and Information	Remarks and references to Appendices
LONGUEVAL	1.10.16	8am	2 Sections improving track North of GINCHY T.13.b and T.7.c. 1 preparing site for Bn. Dump at TRÔNES WOOD.	Ref. Sheet 57 & 2 Edition
"	2.10.16	9am	Nos. 1 and 2 Sections commenced 2 deep dug-outs N of GINCHY for XIV Corps Signals with 100 attached pioneers from 11th Leicesters from 6th D with work to begin carried out in 8 hour reliefs, vertical shafts to lead down to 4 shafts driven along one line — 3'×3'. No 3 Sec. preparing site for Bn. Dump at GUILLEMONT. No 4 " working on track N of GINCHY T.7.c.	
"	3.10.16		1 Sec on dug-outs N.GINCHY. Int. provisionally taken over and now stopped owing to day. 2 Sec on Track No. 4 GINCHY T.c. ½ Sec " constructing shelter for both Batt HQrs at T.8.a.4.4.	
"	4.10.16	8am	2 Sec (1 & 3) on Tracks T.7.c. Rained and no work tried.	
	4pm	2 Sec (2 & 4) with B & D Coys D.L.I. H.Q.s & 2 Assembly Trenches behind front line.	
"	5.10.16	6am	first started GUEDECOURT N.27 d and N.28.c. 3 Secs on other work returned to billets.	
	4pm	No. 1 Sec on work find. 2 Secs on Marlborough making latrines/parapet at T.7 and 6.7.c.	
"	6.10.16	7am	2 Sec (10,3) on Lenin'ght 1 Sec making 2 shelters (6'×9') for advance Bn. HQrs T. N.2.d 1 Platoon D.L.I. making dig-outs to assembly trench.	T.3 Nov. 2nd
	4pm	No 3 Sec. Constructy 2 shelters 12'×8' to advance Ration dumps in T.3a 1.1.4. with 1 Platoon D.L.I. 1 Shelter completed by end of evening. Sec on dug-outs N of GINCHY completed N of Hrt 2 Secs on lightning roads completed work No 4 marked out Track from Bn HQrs 7.8a 4.4 to assembly trench N 27 d. T.3. Nov. 2nd N.9 b 83 a 8 d.	

1577 Wt.W10791/1773 500,000 1/15 D.D.&L. A.D.S.S./Forms/C. 2118.

WAR DIARY
INTELLIGENCE SUMMARY

Army Form C. 2118.

Place	Date	Hour	Summary of Events and Information	Remarks and references to Appendices
LONGUEVAL	7.10.16	2.30p	Advanced parties from Nos 2 and 4 Secs with Battn for an attack on a trench organisation of the position captured. Attack to commence 1.45pm.	At Bazt Coy HQ/Staff zone
		5/-	Nos 1, 3 and 4 Secs moved up. 60th Bde HQrs near GINCHY Station. Rather obscure. Attack on bridge reported, party thro' enemy put. Op. and 2 officers went up to the trenches	
		6.15-	Sappers and party 200 RE's Lgt Role attend	
		8pm	Parties commenced work. 2 Secs and 200 RE's forming up Lgt Rly bolt route forward to right of 61st Bde in CLOUDY TRENCH SE of GUEUDECOURT. 1 Sec and party from No 2 Coy. 100 R.E. working party forming up mg Rly line which consisted of heavy day ballasted existing track to 50 yds N of No 1 Leg Boxes. Work successfully carried through, shell fire heavy. Much opposition for just party brought death later and heavy rain. 1 Sec - (No 3) handed 6 Bn Bde HQrs and what carrying party at 11 pm and wired small portion of front line. 3 Secs (1, 2 and 4) bivouaced to 61st Bde HQrs having orders to relieve 61st Bde park. These sectors returned to their lies carrying party having appeared.	Casualties: 1 Sapper killed 2 Sappers (?) 18 SA(?) 2 ? Approx ? captured by No 3 Sec.
LONGUEVAL	8.10.16	8.30		
	9.10.16	8.30	Division Relieved. Coy marched to camp southside BAZENTIN LE GRAND and BERNAFAY wood. Track roads bridges astride the forward No transport appeared. Arrangements made with French Scyn. French Scys driver and two taken to a safety than Bn. BERNAFAY to SANDPITS Recorded. Recorded as SANDPITS near F19 central Bn. about 3.30 pm	
SANDPITS F.19 central	10.10.16	9a-	Wagons and small party reached from MARICOURT and LONGUEVAL SANDPITS with whole company assembled in camp. Party sent to CITADELLE to take up pontoons which had been captured.	

T.J.Juler Lieut.
o/c 83rd Fd Coy RE

WAR DIARY or INTELLIGENCE SUMMARY

Army Form C. 2118.

(Erase heading not required.)

Instructions regarding War Diaries and Intelligence Summaries are contained in F. S. Regs., Part II. and the Staff Manual respectively. Title Pages will be prepared in manuscript.

[Stamp: 93rd FIELD COMPANY, R.E.]

Place	Date	Hour	Summary of Events and Information	Remarks and references to Appendices
SANDPITS F.19 Central	11/10/16		Rest & refit. Cleaned wagons etc.	ALBERT (Regimental Sheet) 1/40,000 Sheet 62D 1st Edition 1/10000
	12/10/16	10 a.m.	Practice for inspection by 60th Inf. Bde. Group by Coy Commander	
	13/10/16	10.15 a.m.	Inspection of 60th Inf. Bde. Group by Corps Commander, who complimented them on their smart appearance on parade. Rest in comfortable recent good work & them on their smart appearance on parade.	
			Lt near AMIENS (promised)	
			Capt. PENNYCUICK left company with damaged jaw. Command taken over temporarily by Lieut. SCHON. Company rested.	
	14/10/16			
	15/10/16		Marched to DAOURS (Sheet 62D 2nd Edition 1/40,000) toillets N6.d.1.6 via MEAULTE, VILLE-SUR-ANCRE, TREUX, MERICOURT, CORBIE.	
DAOURS	16/10/16		Company rested. } Rifle exercises, physical training & drill for 2 hours each morning	
	17/10/16		Company rested. }	
	18/10/16	5.0 a.m.	Orders received to move to CITADEL (F.21.a ALBERT Sheet) Saffers taken by lorry. Transport marched via several villages as on move on 15th	
CITADEL F.21.a	19/10/16	1 p.m.	Moved to CRATERS (A.8.a). Very wet day. O.C. went one part of proposed pipeline with Lieut. DURHAM R.E. of 14th Corps C.E.'s Staff.	J.R.Allan Lt. RE 9/10/63 —

WAR DIARY — INTELLIGENCE SUMMARY

Army Form C. 2118.

Place	Date	Hour	Summary of Events and Information	Remarks and references to Appendices
CRATERS A8a	20/10/16		Party staked out commencement of proposed pipe-line MONTAUBAN - GUILLEMONT. Sappers drew tools from 8th Divn R.E. Dump at CARNOY. Work on pipe line started in afternoon.	ALBERT Continued Sheet 1/40000
	21/10/16		Work continued on pipe line. Wagons carting material from HAPPY VALLEY SIDING to CRATERS.	
	22/10/16 23/10/16 24		Work continued on pipe line. Work as for 21/10/16.	
	25		Lieut Bennett arrived as reinforcement. 38 men of the more recently joined reinforcements, 6 N.C.O's & men as instructors and 2 Officers went back to CONDÉ to be trained. There were all attached to 94th Fd.Co. R.E. Work continued on pipe line. Remainder of Company carried about 500 yards towards CARNOY.	
	26 27 28 29		Work as on 21/10/16	

J.B.Shan
Capt R.E.
O.C. 83 Fd. Co.R.E.

20th Divisional Engineers

83rd FIELD COMPANY R. E.

NOVEMBER 1 9 1 6

SECRET

Army Form C. 2118.

83 Fd Coy R.E.

WAR DIARY
or
INTELLIGENCE SUMMARY.

Vol 17

(Erase heading not required.)

Place	Date	Hour	Summary of Events and Information	Remarks and references to Appendices
CRATERS (A8a)	30/10		Work continued on pipe line. 52538 2/Cpl BARBER awarded Military Medal, authority 20th Div. order no. dated 26/10/16	ALBERT Combined Sheet 40,000
do	31		Pipe line work continued	
do	Nov. 1		do	
do	2		44392 Sergt. MOLLOY and 115229 A/Sergt. PEPALL awarded Military Medal authority London Gazette dated 27/10/16. Pipe line work continued	
do	3		Pipe line work continued	
do	4		do	
do	5		do	
do	6		Captain MASSIE M.C. arrived to take command of Co. Pipe line work continued.	
do	7		do	
do	8		do	
	9			
	10			
	11		Coy moved by march route to billets at VILLE-SUR-ANCRE & TREUX. T J Shaw Captain in Cmd 83rd Fd Co RE	

Army Form C. 2118.

WAR DIARY
or
INTELLIGENCE SUMMARY.
(Erase heading not required.)

Place	Date	Hour	Summary of Events and Information	Remarks and references to Appendices
	12.		Resting.	
	13.		do	
	14.		Commenced having Mill rifle ranges etc., football	
CORBIE	15		Coy marched to billets at CORBIE & report to "Bde Head.	
	16		Took over R.E. works in CORBIE i.e. New Jewish Baths, Stables etc.	
	17.		R.E. work on Baths, Stables, Theatre & Sawmills.	
	18		do	
	19		Church Parade & took in Cinema Hall	
	20		Coy employed on work at Baths, New Stables, Laundry, Cinema Hall.	
	21		do	
	22			
	23			
	24			
	25			
	26		Church parade for 3 Sections. Work on Laundry continued.	
	27		Work continued on Baths, Stables, the Laundry, Cinema	
	28			
	29			

J.S. Shan
Capt RE
O/c 53 Fd Cy RE

20th Divisional Engineers

83rd FIELD COMPANY R. E.

DECEMBER 1 9 1 6

Army Form C. 2118.

WAR DIARY
or
INTELLIGENCE SUMMARY.

83rd Field Cy. R.E.

SECRET

Vol 18

(Erase heading not required.)

Instructions regarding War Diaries and Intelligence Summaries are contained in F.S. Regs., Part II. and the Staff Manual respectively. Title pages will be prepared in manuscript.

Place	Date	Hour	Summary of Events and Information	Remarks and references to Appendices
CORBIE	30/1/16		Work continued on Stables, Laundry, Baths, & Sawmills	
"	1/2/16		Do	
"	2 "		Drill with Smoke Helmets 7.30am to 9.0am. work continued as above	
"	3 "		Work continued on Stables, Laundry, Baths & Sawmills	
"	4 "		Do	
"	5 "		Do	
"	6 "		Do	
"	7 "		Do	
"	8 "		Do	
"	9 "		Company less No. 3 section marched to TREUX via MERICOURT L'ABBE arriving at 1.30pm. No. 3 section continued work on Laundry at CORBIE.	
TREUX	10 "		Company less No. 3 section marched to TRONES WOOD via MEAULTE, CARNOY and MARICOURT arriving at 4.0pm. Took over camp from 1/3 London Field Co. R.E.	
TRONES WOOD	11		Three sections employed in camp improvements & reconnoitring work.	
"	12		No. 1 Section employed in Left Sector Sust talk. No. 2 on No. 9 Dugouts, No. 3 on Laundry at CORBIE. No. 4 on relieving to GUILLEMONT CAMP.	

Browne Capt RE
OC 83 Fd Cy RE

WAR DIARY
INTELLIGENCE SUMMARY

Army Form C. 2118.

Place: Sheet 2

Date	Hour	Summary of Events and Information	Remarks and references to Appendices
13.		Work continued on Lift. Seln. Duck walk, M.G. and artillery Dugouts. GUILLEMONT CAMP.	
14&15		do	
16.		Work continued on M.G. + Arty Dugouts, Extension to GUILLEMONT CAMP. - Commenced cleaning Strong Point at T.9.6.9.7.	
17.		Work continued on M.G. and Arty Dugouts, new Duck walk & OZONE commenced. Drainage of Strong Points T.9.6.9.7 and T.3.2.3.6. continued, also work on Sock-drying shed + GUILLEMONT CAMP.	
18th 19. 20.		do	
21st 22 – 23rd		Digging intermediate line + making Strong Point.	
24" 4-30		A.M. Paraded. No 2 & 1 Sections march to BONFAY FARM, for work cleaning, hutting, making roads etc. No. 1 + 4 Sections to CRATERS near MONTAUBAN for work on improvement + extensions to camps etc.	

Major
O.C. 73rd Field Coy.

War Diary
of the
85nd Field Company R.E.

January 1917

SECRET

Army Form C. 2118.

Instructions regarding War Diaries and Intelligence Summaries are contained in F.S. Regs., Part II. and the Staff Manual respectively. Title pages will be prepared in manuscript.

WAR DIARY
or
INTELLIGENCE SUMMARY.
(Erase heading not required.)

83rd Fd. Co. R.E.

Place	Date	Hour	Summary of Events and Information	Remarks and references to Appendices
CRATERS	31/76/77		Nos 1 & 4 sections continued work on camps.	
BRONFAY FM.	do do		" 2 & 3 " drawing gensions of huts etc	
	2/77		Nos 1 & 4 sections by route march to WEDGEWOOD. Nos 2 & 3 sections & H.Q. by route march to WEDGEWOOD area MARICOURT, TRONES WOOD, & GUILLEMONT. Took over camp from 555 Fd Co RE also work. Work in hand at CRATERS and BRONFAY FARM handed over to 55th Fd. Co. RE.	
	3			
	3rd to 26th		1 section on RE advanced B.D.g & New Zealand Div. Sections worked on Boot Exchange and Drying Room at HAIEWOOD	
WEDGE WOOD			do do completing same on 26.	
			do do advanced billets in COMBLES until the 11th when this was taken over by the Guards Division	
			do do wiring intermediate line also M.C.E. making dug outs &	
			do do improving camp, building 4 huts, 1 medical inspection room, 1 bath house, also stalls for horses.	B.I.b.8 & sheet ALBERT continued
			No 1 section attached to 8th Fd. Co. RE from 21st to 26th. MAJOR I.W. MASSIE, M.C. R.E. proceeded to RE School LE PARCQ on 11th	

J. Murray Major.
O.C. 83rd Fd Co RE

WAR DIARY
INTELLIGENCE SUMMARY.
(Erase heading not required.)

Army Form C. 2118.

Place	Date	Hour	Summary of Events and Information	Remarks and references to Appendices
WEDGE WOOD	27th		Company proceeded by route march to MEAULTE via GUILLEMONT, TRONES WOOD, MONTAUBAN and MAMETZ.	
MEAULTE	28th		Company proceeded by route march to HEILLY via VILLE-RIBEMONT.	E.16.d.6.1.
HEILLY	29th		Company rested	
	30th		Work commenced on hos 36 & 38 C.C.S.	

J. Munro
Major
O.C. 130th Co. R.E.

WAR DIARY
— or —
INTELLIGENCE SUMMARY

Army Form C. 2118.

S3 3rd Army SECRET Vol 20

(Erase heading not required.)

Place	Date	Hour	Summary of Events and Information	Remarks and references to Appendices
HEILLY	31/7 to 6/7		Sections worked on erection of huts at 36 and 38 C.C.S.	
	7/7		One section training	
S.30.a.	8/7		Coy. conveyed by busses to TRONES WOOD via RIBEMONT, BUIRE, DERNANCOURT, MEAULTE and MONTAUBAN. Camp taken over from 455th West Riding Fd. Co. R.E. at S.30.a. No 1 section erecting huts cookhouses etc in Camp. dugouts reconnoitred for advanced accommodation for 2 sections. No 2 section working on strong Point B. T.10.b.9.5. 3 sections working in forward area on deep dug outs duckwalks etc. Nos 3 & 4 sections moved to advanced billets at T.16.a.6.7	
	9/7 to 10/7		Work carried on in forward area by 3 sections on deep dug outs duckwalks etc. Relieved of forward work by 84th Fd Co R.E. Back work taken over from 84th Fd Co R.E. No 1 section marched to CARNOY for work in camps	
	16/7		Nos 3 & 4 sections rejoined Coy at S.30.a	
	17/7 to 27/7		No 2 section miscellaneous camp work on Camps near BRIQUETRIE. No 3 section renewing accomodation at large deep dugout S.W. of GUILLEMONT. No 4 section work on Camps near GUILLEMONT Station.	

WAR DIARY

INTELLIGENCE SUMMARY.
(Erase heading not required.)

Army Form C. 2118.

Vol 21

Added 57 & 58 W. FRAME

Place	Date	Hour	Summary of Events and Information	Remarks and references to Appendices
	28/7/17 to 1/8/17		General work on camps in rear Dunl. area continued	
	2/8/17 to 7/8/17		Work in rear Dunl. area handed over to 96th Fd. Co. R.E. Nos 1 and 2 sections marched to forward billets and took over work from 96th Fd. Co. R.E. in forward area. Work continued on deep dugouts, duckwalks, M.G.E's etc.	
	8/8/17		Work in forward area handed over to 96th Fd. Co. R.E. Nos. 1 and 2 sections rejoined H.Qrs at S.30.a.5.5.	
	9/8/17 to 13/8/17		Sections training under section officers. Work continued on Buckingham Palace, Dunl. Baths etc.	
	14/8/17 to 16/8/17		Nos 3 and 4 sections marched to forward billets and took over work from 84th Fd. Co. R.E. in forward area. Work continued on deep dugouts, duckwalks, M.G.E's etc.	
	17/8/17 to 20/8/17		No 3 section worked under orders of 60th Brigade, searching dugouts. No 4 section attached to 96th Fd. Co. R.E. remainder worked on mule tracks, and duck walks, shelters for O.Ms headquarters at Bovril Trench commenced.	
	21/8/17 to 22/8/17		Nos 1 and 2 sections marched to forward billets at T.16.a.8.7. No 3 section rejoined H.Qrs at S.30.a.5.5.	

JM Morris
Major RE
OC 83rd Fd Co RE

Army Form C. 2118.

WAR DIARY
INTELLIGENCE SUMMARY.
(Erase heading not required.)

Instructions regarding War Diaries and Intelligence Summaries are contained in F. S. Regs., Part II. and the Staff Manual respectively. Title pages will be prepared in manuscript.

Place	Date	Hour	Summary of Events and Information	Remarks and references to Appendices
	23/3/17		H.Qrs and No 3 section moved to forward billets at T.17.d.5.5. Nos 1 and 2 sections rejoined H.Qrs at T.17.d 55.	Aubigny au Bac FRANCE
	24/3/17 to 26/3/17		No 2 section worked on erecting tents at U10.c.5.6 for company. No 1 section wiring, remainder working in camp.	
	27/3/17		Nos 1 and 2 sections moved forward to tents at U.10.c.5.6 Bridge at V2.d 9.8 (CANAL DU NORD) made passable.	
	28/3/17		No 2 section moved forward to ETRICOURT. work on roads, camps, etc.	
	29/3/17		H.Qrs and transport moved to camp at U.10.c.5.6.	

J Munro
Major RE
OC 63RD Fd Coy RE

WAR DIARY
INTELLIGENCE SUMMARY

Army Form C. 2118.

83rd Coy R.E.

Sheet 57 E
FRANCE

Place	Date	Hour	Summary of Events and Information	Remarks and references to Appendices
	30/3/17		H.Qrs, No 3 section and transport marched to billets at LECHELLE. P.25.c.3.3. No 1 section marched to billets at ETRICOURT.	
	31/3/17 to 1/4/17		Work on clearing roads, water points, wiring and repairing billets. Nos 1 and 2 sections rejoined H.Qrs at LECHELLE. 4 & 4 section rejoined 1/4/17.	
	2/4/17 to 13/4/17		Work on clearing roads, water points, wiring, strong points, searching for mines and traps and repairing billets. Enemy machine gun explored by Sgt Rgt BEE W and L/Cpl. REED E. at attack on METZ-EN-COUTURE 4.4.17. The following were received from HQ 60th Brigade 13.4.17. "The B.G.C. wishes to thank and congratulate all ranks of 83rd Field C.B. R.E. for the excellent work both on digging and wiring which they have done on various places during the last tour in the 64th front line". Work on rear area taken over from 91st Fd Co R.E.	
	14/4/17		Work on forward area handed over to 91st Fd Co R.E. Sections concentrated on billets, roads, water points, strong points and wiring.	
	15/4/17 to 19/4/17		Work on billets, roads, water points and wiring, bridging on pontooning and heavy bridging.	
	20/4/17 to 29/4/17		Work in forward area taken over from 84th Fd Co R.E. Work on rear area handed over to 84th Fd Co R.E. Sections moved to billets at METZ-EN-COUTURE Q.19.d.7.9. as follows, No 3 section 21.4.17, No 2 section 23.4.17, No 1 section 25.4.17, H.Q. 26.4.17. Work on wiring, erecting screens, repairing billets, dismantling German huts, clearing roads, water points and searching for mines & traps. Honours & Rewards. Under authority granted by His Majesty the King the Corps Commander awards the Military Medal to 48835 Sgt. W.BEE 49772 Cpl. J. HAMILTON 48840 L/Cpl E. REED 25.4.17.	

J. [signature]
Major, R.E.
Comdg. 83rd Fd. Co. R.E.

SECRET   Sheet -1

83rd Field Coy, R.E.

WAR DIARY or INTELLIGENCE SUMMARY
(Erase heading not required.)

Army Form C. 2118.
May. 1917
Vol 23

Place	Date	Hour	Summary of Events and Information	Remarks and references to Appendices
METZ-EN-COUTURE.	1st–12th		Coy. throughout Company. 7 Officers 211 O.R. During time of 12 days in the line, a new front line was pushed out from our trench to 30 yds in front. Older line in MARETT was turned and deep fire trench 3'6" deep and 6'ft wide built throughout the whole 40th Bde. front. It from Q.3.6.3.3 to Q.11.6.6.2 about 3000 yds. A fire step of work by the infantry under R.E. supervision. The front line not-well sited being almost throughout now work in forward area to 96th Field Coy, + 67th new [from] B/Trescault + Bilhem R.E. took over work in reserve. Company marched to billets at YTRES. P.2.6.a.9.5.	2067/1 2.6.17
DESSART WOOD. W.1.6.2.4.	13th		40th Div: following received:- The Divisional Commander under his congratulations conveys to 83rd Field Coy, R.E. 229 Field Coy. R.E. inducted to DESSART WOOD yesterday Feb 13 inst. During tour of 5 days in the line front, line was re-sited + pushed forward to 300 yds from our front. 60th Bde. front running in front. J/Beaucamp #4 [being] really throughout the whole length. Look done by infantry under R.E. supervision. Old front line repaired mostly by me labour by 96th + R/Beaucamp R.E. Relieved by 429th Field Coy, R.E. & marched to billets in YTRES. □ Villers-Plouich by 40th Divn. Company marched to billets at LE TRANSLOY 0.31.a.7.7.	
	22nd		" " " FAVREUIL H16.c.5.4.	
	23rd		" " " Villers at H.12.a.7.6. Being transferred from	
	24th		Fourth to Fifth Army	
	25th		Company marched to billets at H.12.a.7.6 & took over work in line from 14th Australian Field Coy. R.E.	

"SECRET"   SHEET. 2.

WAR DIARY
or
INTELLIGENCE SUMMARY

83rd Field Coy. R.E.

Army Form C. 2118.

Place	Date	Hour	Summary of Events and Information	Remarks and references to Appendices
H.16.b.5.4.	23rd (contd)	by 60th Bde.	Front line between BULLECOURT and LAGNICOURT. Left flank in C.11.a (HINDENBURG LINE at U.23.c.9.1. (Sheet 57B 1/40,000). right flank in trench at C.11.a.2.3. (Sheet 57c. 1/40,000).	Sheet 57c 1/40,000
	26th		Work commenced on front-slopping & widening front line trench throughout also strong thinning wire.	
			These sections moved up & dug in at C.16.b.2.3. working tribes being too far back.	
	27th 4.30 pm		Work mostly making dust dugouts. Splendid progress. No. 1 & 2 Advance Dumps. Bayone HQ Coy. Batts. A & B. also repairing & pairing pumps in 3 wells in NOREUIL.	
C.20.a.00. VRAUCOURT.	30th		HQ Coy + 3 sections concentrated in new advance billet at C.20.a.00. in front of VRAUCOURT. Transport remained at H.12.a.7.6. Casualties during the month	
			Officers (Army) — Killed Wounded	
			O.R. 7. — 1	
			Awards Mentioned in Despatches.	
			" Lt. T.A. SMITH. 83rd Field Coy R.E. Gazette May 15 1917. (Comds 83rd Field Coy R.E.)	
			No 4.6200. 2Cpl. C. WILSON do.	

JMcCane
Major
Comdg. 83rd Field Coy R.E.

WAR DIARY
or
INTELLIGENCE SUMMARY

Army Form C. 2118.

93 "I.W.S." Coy R.E.

Place	Date	Hour	Summary of Events and Information	Remarks and references to Appendices
	31/5		No.2 section returned to rear billet at H.12.a.4.6.	Sheet 57.C N.W. France
	1/6		Co. H Qrs at H.12.a.4.6.	
	4/6		Work in Left Brigade Section of Dund Front	
	5/6		Standard over-work on Left Brigade section to 96th Sa. Co. R.E. and by concentrated in back billet H.12.a.4.6. near BEUGNATRE	
	6/6		General clean up	
	7/6			
	10/6		3 Sections on R.E. works. 1 Section training.	
	12/6			
	13/6		H.Q. No 2 & 4 sections moved to advanced billets at C9ga 5.1 and took over work from 84 & 21 Co. R.E. Once section employed on main line of resistance and two sections on tunnel dugouts.	
			On the left 59th Inf Bde on the right 144 Inf Bde.	
			Front line held by series of posts. Work. Line of wire. no support line except a few posts interconnected line a series of T gaps off sunken road	
	14/6 to 25/6		During tour in the line one section supervised work on making Reserve Line, a series of T gaps connected-up throughout by 4'6" x 3' trench requires deepening revetting two sections employed on deep dugouts with revetting overhang parties. good progress inside.	
	25/26		Relieved by 460 & 561 Co. R.E. 62nd Divn and Coy concentrated at Rear Billet	
	26/6		Coy marched to billets at HERMIES-LE-PETIT G.14.a.6.9.	
	27/6		Cleaning up and settling in	
	28/6 to 29/6		Coy training, squad drill, physical training exercises and recreational training	
			Transport of Coy marched to ACHEUX en route for CANAPLES	
			Co. strength on 31/5 = 213 29/6 = 209 Casualties during month 1 OR killed 2 OR wounded Co. Rfd. CPLS.

2449 Wt. W14957/M90 750,000 1/16 J.B.C. & A. Forms/C.2118/12

Major R.E.
Commanding 93rd I.W.S. Coy R.E.

WAR DIARY or INTELLIGENCE SUMMARY

Army Form C. 2118.

SECRET

83 "J" Coy R.E.

Place	Date	Hour	Summary of Events and Information	Remarks and references to Appendices
ACHIET-LE-PETIT	30/6/17		Coy less transport marched from ACHIET-LE-PETIT and entrained at ACHIET-LE-GRAND at 8.30 a.m. en route for CHARPLES. Detrained at CANDAS at 11.30 a.m. and marched to CHARPLES arriving at 1.0 p.m. Transport arrived at 4.0 p.m.	
CHARPLES	1/7/17		Church Parade. Coy rested	REF. LENS 11 1/100,000
do	2/7/17 to 7/17		Coy paraded at 6.45 a.m. and went for short route march for acclimatisation of R.C.O's on drill etc. commenced. General Training commenced in Physical exercises, squad drill, section drill and Coy drill. Lectures given on reconnoitering, musketry and standing orders. Coy inspected by O.C. 20th Divn on 4/7/17	
HALLOY-LES-PERNOIS	8/7/17		Coy and transport moved to billets at HALLOY-LES-PERNOIS	
TIRANCOURT	9/7/17		Coy (and platoon equipment) marched to billets at TIRANCOURT	
do	10/7/17 to 12/7/17		Training in Pontooning on river SOMME carried out.	
HALLOY-LES-PERNOIS	13/7/17 to 19/7/17		Coy returned to HALLOY-LES-PERNOIS on night of 12/7/17	
do	20/7/17		Training in extended order drill, map reading, use of compass and knots and lashings. Coy were instructed in bombing at 60th Batt. Bombing school on 16.7.17. 2 Officers and 100 infantry joined Coy on 17/7/17. Coy and transport inspected by C.R.E. 20th Divn on 18/7/17	REF. HAZEBROUCK 5A
E.17.d.6.4	21/7/17		Coy and transport paraded at 9.0 a.m and marched to DOULLENS arriving at 2.0 a.m. and entrained. Detrained at HOPOUTRE at 12 m.n. and marched to E.17.d.6.4 arriving at 2.30 a.m	
do	22/7/17 to 29/7/17		General Training	
	30/7/17		Coy moved to CANADA FARM (J.14.28) A.16.	

J. Marsh(?)
Major R.E.
O.C. 83rd J. Coy. R.E.

WAR DIARY or **INTELLIGENCE SUMMARY**

Army Form C. 2118.

83 Fd Coy
SECRET.

August 1917

Place	Date	Hour	Summary of Events and Information	Remarks and references to Appendices
BOESINGHE	July 31		Offensive Operations. Coy employed on making plank roadway across the YSER CANAL	Sheet 28 N.W.
	August 1st to 5th		Plank road way continued to HUDDLESTON CROSS ROADS	
	6th 7th		Coy moved to CANAL BANK near ESSEX FARM Rd.	
	8th to 16th		Coy employed on making DECAUVILLE Ry to STRAY FARM. Preparation of battle dumps of R.E. Materials 200 yds N.E. of IRON CROSS.	
	16th 17th		Offensive Operations. Coy employed on two stong points near LANGEMARCK. Placing foot bridges across the STEEN BEEK.	
			Blowing up dug-outs at the IGN SITE.	
	18th		Coy moved to DAWSONS CORNER DECAUVILLE railway Camp.	
	19th		Coy moved SUTTON CAMP in the S.1 AREA.	
	20th to 30th		Clearing up. General training. Construction of two 30 yard. Trussel bridges	
	31st		Moved at 5.30 P.M. to WHITE HOPE COR for work on roads made O.E.	

WAR DIARY
or
INTELLIGENCE SUMMARY

SECRET.

83 Fd Coy Army Form C. 2118.
83rd Field Coy, R.E.

Place	Date	Hour	Summary of Events and Information	Remarks and references to Appendices
Wieltje Corner	1st Sept to 6 Sept	—	Strength 8 Offrs 6 O.R. 192. Attd. Inf. Offrs 6 O.R. 199. Coy employed under C.E. 16th Corps making plank roads in forward area through old German filled system & repairing metal roads destroyed by shell fire.	
	7 Sept		Moved by train to Saulsan [?] Camp, near Crombeke for rest.	
Canal Bank near Boesinghe	10 Sept		Returned to forward area by train. Artillery on Canal Bank near Boesinghe. Relieved 121st Field Coy. R.E. 38th Welsh Division & work in the line and both over bombing parties of Cavalry (R.Lancey) of 4th Dragoon Guards & 6th 4th D.G. Gunners took over duties in front of Langemarck, 51st Division on its right, Guards Divn on its left flank.	
	11th to 19th Sept		Preparations for Minor operation. Repair relaying of tramlines & forward dumps at Goldfish Farm and to French forward positions in Steenbeek Valley. Marking out "Jumping off" positions for infantry & trench shelters close to outpost line for attack on Eagle and Langemarck trenches. It Wayman severely wounded in this operation.	
	20th Sept		60th Bde attack, 83rd Fd Coy were attached, attacked at dawn. Company detailed to make three strong points in captured area. Strong points in this operation, no attack was unsuccessful, left up in the centre at safety truck. Three strong points made in Captured line.	
	21st to 26th Sept		Returned to work under CRE on communication work on tramway & plank lines & want to front line in Steenbeek valley. Making new Bavarian Bt. Canal Bank and trench lines between this in area of Ferm [illegible] (Returned).	

SECRET
Part II

WAR DIARY
or
INTELLIGENCE SUMMARY
(Erase heading not required.)

Army Form C. 2118.

B. July 16, 1918

Place	Date	Hour	Summary of Events and Information	Remarks and references to Appendices
	27/5/18		Company + attached infantry moved by train to S.I. arm, billetted at Sablon Camp. Relieved by 406 Inft.A.Cy, A.I.F. "Division."	
	28th 29/5/18		Rest + training.	
	29/5/18		During this tour of duty in the line casualties were heavy, mainly suffered working in forward area of communication. Enemy bombed by himself. This principally came from shelling + bombing. Enemy aerial bombing activity, particularly at night, very marked. Strength 7 Coy. Off. 6 – O.R. 214. attd. 2 off. Off. 2. O.R. 106. Casualties during the month. Off. – Killed – 1. O.R. – 7 – 28. Wounded. Awards. L/Cpl. C. Thompson no 46665. Awarded Military Medal for gallantry in assisting infantry attack on Rue Bonfile, he was in charge of a party of sappers with explosives to blow in concrete dugouts, many fournaux saucisses while charges were being placed. Pte H. Baker no 61070 awarded military medal for gallantry when taking up R.E. stores. His mo was killed. His other drivers wounded. You horses killed under heavy shell fire, he took charge and finally made + brought his party away.	

J. Howard
Lieutenant
B. Field Cy RE

WAR DIARY or INTELLIGENCE SUMMARY

Army Form C. 2118.
83rd FIELD COMPANY, R.E.
SECRET.

Place	Date	Hour	Summary of Events and Information	Remarks and references to Appendices
SALEM CAMP	30/9		Strength of Coy. Officers 6 O.Rs. 244	
	1/10		Rest and Training.	
	2"		Marched to PROVEN Ry train en route for BAPAUME	Sheet 57C
	3"		Arrived BAPAUME marched to camp at BARASTRE.	
	4"		Rest Training	
	5"		Moved by route march to billet in SOREL.	
	6"/10		Marched to billets as follows Nos 1 & 3 sections en forward billet at Q.24.c.2 & 7 Q.24.c.26	
15"			Nos 2,4 & H.Q. sections Q.34.c.4.5. Transport Lines W7.b.6.8 Work over cont. in two [?] from 23/10 sd Co RE	
			Nos 1 & 3 sections organising maintenance of trenches on their respective battalion areas leading from Fort Blair, Gorge Katsheno Sand Drying Rooms. No 4 section working underground dugout near BEET FACTORY near BEAUCAMP. No 2 section laying the road area.	
	17"		H.Qrs & No 4 section moved to Advanced billets in TRESCAULT ROAD.	
	18" to 25"		Nos 1 & 3 sections working on the line, working & making shelters & garrisons of posts. No 4 working on water supply etc No 2 making accommodation on TRESCAULT ROAD.	
	26" to 30"		No 2 section moved to Advanced Billets and relieved No 1 section of work on the road. No 1 section moved to forward lines. Light breakfast joined the by Egt. Heqs. lines. Transferred to 96 N Zl Co R.E.	
			[lengthy paragraph of notes]... 5.9" shell ... 12" ... 2 C.W.G. Stokes & Cleave shot 1 M.M. [signatures]	

Strength of Coy. 7 officers 213 O.Rs. Casualties for month Nil. 2Cpl Stokes & Cleave shot.

WAR DIARY or INTELLIGENCE SUMMARY

Army Form C. 2118.

83 Fd Coy R.E.

SECRET

Place	Date	Hour	Summary of Events and Information	Remarks and references to Appendices
	3/11/17 to 6/11/17		Strength of Coy. 1.11.17. 4 Officers 212 ORs Attd only 2 Officers 194 ORs. Work normal. No 2 & 3 sections working with Battalions in the line. No 4 section BEAUCAMP water supply, Lookouts, artillery OPs, Trench mortar emplacements and making dugouts in Company Billet TRESCAULT road. No 1 section putting up track area.	Sheet 57⅓
	7/11/17 to 16/11/17		Lt Mulhollow & Sgt Molloy 9th Bn. Albans running Bde Field Works School. No 1 section relieved No 3 section of work in Left Batln Sector. No 3 section moved to Horse Lines. Coy employed making shelter accommodation	
	17/11/17 to 19/11/17		Coy less No 3 section hauled over work and billets to London Rd. Co Hd Qrs. No 1 Section Dum and moved to billets in HEUDICOURT. No 3 section carried on work on Durl forward area making tracks in Tanks across railway, lumber roads and trenches and pot 13. Artillery trigaux. Also across trenches.	
	20/11/17		Company less No 3 section moved to VILLERS PLOUCH. No 3 section attached 166th Inf Bde for attack. Sheet Company successfully attacked HINDENBURG LINE between LA VACQUERIE and CAMBRAI RAILWAY on	COUZEUCOURT
	21/11/17 22/11/17 23/11/17		Lt. Reeve's Company employed on making tracks through HINDENBURG LINE clearing wire and digging trenches, also reconstructing tryboring up station supply. Continued work on tracks on water supply.	
	24/11/17 to 29/11/17		3 sections employed on carrying new Bde Front from G.33 d.9.6. G.32 d.9.0. (about COUZEUCOURT) 1500 yards of fence wound front that up. No 3 section employed in organizing, reinforcing digging trenches along 6th Bde Front, also making strong points of cemetery at G.34 d.6.8. No ½ section employed on making shelters in earths and sunken roads in Bde forward area. No 1 & 4 sections employed on making new billets for Coy and DivH.H.Q.	

Strength of Coy. 29.11.17. 4 Officers 216 ORs Attd Inf. 2 Officers 194 ORs
Casualties during month 1 OR died of wounds 1 OR wounded

J. Murray
Major RE
Comdg 83rd Fd Co R.E.

WAR DIARY or INTELLIGENCE SUMMARY

Army Form C. 2118.

SECRET Sheet 1. 83' Field Coy. R.E.

Place	Date	Hour	Summary of Events and Information	Remarks and references to Appendices
VILLERS-PLOUICH Inf. LENS. II	30th Aus		O/S O.R. 83' field Coy. R.E. 240. 2. 10.4 Batt. infantry. Enemy developed heavy attack on our own on Right Flank necessitating withdrawal on right flank of our Divisional front. Transport ordered further back. Transport to Camp near FINS. Nos 2 & 3 Sections alarmed in their forward billets when OUSMET FARM shelling after light work. 2 moving billets of a new position their billets being completely outflanked, they became involved in its fighting between LATEAU WOOD – LONGAVESNES. Casualties Lt. L.B. LEE missing, last seen carrying a wounded man on his back. Lt. A.M. HAY wounded at duty. 9 O.R. wounded, 12 O.R. missing. 1 O.R. wounded & missing. Nos 1 Section with reception B after & Shelter equipment, Nos 2 & 3 Section lost all their equipment including kits lost etc. Remainder J.G. H.Q. Nos 1 & 4 Section with attached infantry moved to H. in Gouzeaucourt Ravine & thence FUSILIER TRENCH in front of VILLERS-PLOUICH. Enemy attack continued. Coy ordered to move to DUN RAVEN TRENCH at 7am & situation in Coy. with army GOMMECOURT. Trench shelled during afternoon. Casualties, 2 O.R. killed. 2 O.R. wounded. at 10 pm 4/5 field Coy arrived and orders to relieve 83 field Coy. + 83 fd Coy to proceed to billets at SOREL.	
SOREL	2"		Coy noted at SOREL.	
	3"		Marched to KYTREL & entrained for BUIRE then marched to billets at MARMYET. Transport proceeded by road to MEAULTE.	

Army Form C. 2118.

WAR DIARY or INTELLIGENCE SUMMARY Sheet II

(Erase heading not required.)

Place	Date	Hour	Summary of Events and Information	Remarks and references to Appendices
VARENNES	4"		Coy Hrs transport active #	
	5"		Coy lers transport commenced refitting. Transport proceeded by road to AMPLIER. Men hopers entrained to entrain which remained at MERVILLE.	
	6"		Coy lers Transport marched to AVELUY to entrain for HESDIN & then marched to MARENLA. Transport marched to PILLIEVRES.	
GOURNAY	7"		Coy lers transport marched to GOURNAY, Transport rejoined Coy.	
			Coy resting & trained	
			Coy lers transport moved to LE CROCQUET (near BLARINGHEM) by bus, transport by road.	
Inf HAZEBROUCK	9" 6-12"			
	11" 13"		Rest & training at LE CROCQUET	
LE CROQUET	14" 16 16"		Coy less transport marched to STRAZEELE on 16". Transport moved by train.	
R.E. FARM	17"		Coy ordered forward to work under C.E. IX Corps. Coy less transport moved by train to DICKEBUSCH & marched to billets at R.E. FARM, near KEMMEL	
near KEMMEL			Transport rejoined Coy.	
	18"		Training	
	19"		Reconnoitering work on which Coy is to be employed i.e. Corps Defence line running in front of MONT SOREL — HEDGE ST TUNNELS — TOR TOP TUNNELS — STIRLING CASTLE.	
	20" & 25"		Employed in carrying forward material to new New Corps Defence line Carrying party — 6" K.S.L.I. (350. O.R.) 2 Coys 11" D.L.I. (120. O.R.) wiring work N.B. proceeded with on account of very hard frost. 6" K.S.L.I. & 2 coys 11"D.L.I. commenced wiring under supervision of 7 F.S. 3"d Coy.	

WAR DIARY or INTELLIGENCE SUMMARY

Army Form C. 2118.

Place	Date	Hour	Summary of Events and Information	Remarks and references to Appendices
R.E. FARM. NEAR KEMMEL	24th		Sappers & D.L.I. but no infantry, finished front belt of Corps line were, except 500 x on extreme left. Left out left corps on left had settled their line.	
	28th		9 Reinforcements (1 driver & 8 sappers) joined Coy. 3 appears very poor class of men. Collected pontoon equipment from OUDERDOM.	
	29th		Sappers & D.L.I. & 1/1 K.R.R.B. working on corps line eung on 2nd belt, and finishing front belt on left across MENIN ROAD. 2450 x completed by Coy & 11 K.D.L.I. 11 K.R.B. carrying.	
	30th		16 wagon loads of wiring material carted to PLUMMER'S DUMP on morning & carried to Corps line wire at night by 11 K.R.B. D.L.I. wired 300 x of 2nd belt. Pontoons of 96 2nd Co. R.E. brought from OUDERDOM RAILHEAD Cable Coy. D.L.I. & 11 K.R.B. wiring 3rd belt of Corps line wire. 2,700 x completed.	
	30th		Coy strength 7 Officers 195 O.Rs. Casualties during month :- OFFICERS 1 missing 1 Wounded at duty. ORs 8 Wounded 1 Wounded missing 12 missing 1 Wounded at duty. 2 Killed } attached 3 Wounded } infantry	

Ruttledge Capt. RE.
OC 83rd Fd. Co. R.E.

WAR DIARY
or
SECRET INTELLIGENCE SUMMARY
(Erase heading not required.)

Army Form C. 2118.

1st Bn 7th C? [?]

SHEET 1. Vol 31

Place	Date	Hour	Summary of Events and Information	Remarks and references to Appendices
Re Return near MENIN	31st Dec 6.5/16		Contd any important work on MENIN Corps main Line of Defence from MENIN ROAD to STIRLING CASTLE and MOUNT SOREL.	
JHENDAM TUNNELS 29.6.8.9.	1st Jan		Relieved 2nd "D" Field Coy RE at JASPER TUNNELS on left frontage just N of ZILLEBEKE near MENIN ROAD. Here lines at KRUISSTRAAT near DIKKEBUSCH A2. A3. and A50.	
	7+8.		Settling in, general mess work. 2 sections on Bank mine work, looking on general duckwalk tracks. Left Batln M.G. Emplacements built on MENIN ROAD.	
	9th 10.13.		Army Head Lines of Resistance - Improvements to tunnels, deflecting walls - loopholes, improvements to billets at ZWARN CHATEAU and constructing shelters at HORNBY SIDINGS. No. 3 Section relieved No 4 Section of work in present mine dog houses & mine lines & 6th own work and work.	
	14.		Army Rear Line of Resistance. Making Byrne [?] Road to Post Road [?] No 2 Section relieved No 1 Section of fourgasse mines, covering the [?] posts.	
	15th 16 17".		Making a shell proof [?] Post. They also through & now mostly done setting [?] fougasses installed. line (reconn'd) and improvements from [?] & the tunnels relined & covered ways. A fourgasse installed, new work to [?] mine [?] & new [?] & drainage. Eml of payer Libery round points in	
	20.		Reserve Line [?] by [?] up, [?] shell hole, a few ? and various work.	
	21st 22 23".		A.T.P. A [?] successful shoot. Bomb Punte & stokes [?] accounted & reinforced observers, two Lewis Gun & Servis [?] installed. Very much Zone of [?] Punte installed firing to commune different [?] [?] desservant [?] in [?] [?]	

WAR DIARY or INTELLIGENCE SUMMARY

83rd Field Coy R.E.
SHEET II

Army Form C. 2118.

Place	Date	Hour	Summary of Events and Information	Remarks and references to Appendices
Packhorse Tunnels	27 Jan		No 4 Section relieved No 3 & took in forward area & left one section back. Area as before, making 2 huts for Lewis gun Equipment, shelters at Forward AMMO /m ammunition, drainage of FORRESTER CAMP etc.	
	29 to 30		Evidence took just commenced the laying, burying lifting trench and conducting strong points in HARE & KEEP Reserve Lines. Rea. Section employed on dummy FORRESTER CAMP and executing YMCA hut etc.	
	30 Jan		Coy Strength: 5 Officers, 187 O.R. 2 Men newly promoted from L/Cpl during the month. 1 Officer wounded. Ga/Lt/T. McKerrin of 70 O.R. wounded during the month in Shakespeare ground Coy 25/1/17.	

J. Howard Major RE
83rd Field Coy R.E.

Army Form C. 2118.

SECRET

WAR DIARY
or
INTELLIGENCE SUMMARY

83rd Field Coy R.E.
SHEET 1

(Erase heading not required.)

Place	Date	Hour	Summary of Events and Information	Remarks and references to Appendices
KROMSTRAAT. near DICKEBUSCH (Shet. HAZEBROUCK) 5A.	3rd Jan. to 9th Feb.		Company working in Infantry Area in "POLDERHOEK SECTOR" of Divisional Front. Two sections on duct work, two sections on back area work.	
	3rd Feb.		No.1 Section relieved No.2 of work in forward area, relaying & renewing foul. & duckboard tracks, including BODY & HELL-AVE. No.2 Section moves to back area work on Infcar. Huts. trucking huneuttali etc.	
	8th Feb.		No 4 Section moves to HALFWAY HOUSE near ZILLEBEKE but later was work on one Battalion front from newly-formed Divisional infantry Divisional front on the left K POLYGONBEEK & REUTELBEEK. took mainly cutting & renewing Reserve Line & Support Line.	
	10th Feb.		No 3 Section relieve No 4 on line of work in forward area	
	13th Feb.		Attached infantry repair 1st unit ment at MLBERTA CAMP (12" K.R.R.C.) No 1 & 3 Sections had own work in line to Division & 37 "Division & transport completed moves	
			to STRAZEELE.	
RACQUINGHEM. 16th Feb. (HAZEBROUCK 5A)			Company Hd Transport moved by train from DICKEBUSCH to EBBLYNGHEM & hence to billets at RACQUINGHEM. Transport reported arrival to Company.	
	17th-19th Feb.		Training. Friday equipment returned to Company.	
	20th Feb.		Learning. Section Drill, musketry, Physical Training, Company Drill, Officers & Serjts.	
	21st Feb.		Company marches complete to STEENBECQUE & entrained at 1pm for NESLE.	

449 Wt. W14957/M90 750,000 1/16 J.B.C. & A. Forms/C.2118/12.

Army Form C. 2118.

SECRET

WAR DIARY
or
INTELLIGENCE SUMMARY

83rd Jul B C, B
Sheet 11

(Erase heading not required.)

Instructions regarding War Diaries and Intelligence Summaries are contained in F. S. Regs., Part II. and the Staff Manual respectively. Title Pages will be prepared in manuscript.

Place	Date	Hour	Summary of Events and Information	Remarks and references to Appendices
ERCHEU Nr AMIENS	22nd Feb		Company arrived NESLE 3.30 a.m.	
	23rd-27th Feb.		Engineers training. Coy Strength 40 Officers 196 O.R. Lt F.H. POOLE joined Coy on 26/2/15.	J. Moray Major RE OC "Leeds" Coy

2449 Wt. W14957/M90 750,000 1/16 J.B.C. & A. Forms/C.2118/12.

20th Divisional Engineers

83rd FEILD COMPANY R. E.

M A R C H 1 9 1 8

WAR DIARY or INTELLIGENCE SUMMARY

Army Form C. 2118.

(Erase heading not required.)

2nd/4th Bn. R. Berks. St. Quentin and Amiens 1/100,000 — B.E.F. France 20

Place	Date	Hour	Summary of Events and Information	Remarks and references to Appendices
ERCHEU	1st March		Company training - making rifle range & bayonet fighting area for 60" Bde.	
SOMMETTE EAUCOURT	3rd		Company moved to SOMMETTE-EAUCOURT. Lens No.1 Section to HAM & No.3 Sect. to ANNOIS. Remainder work on Rear Zone Defences.	
	4th		Commenced work on Rear Zone Defences.	
	5th-13th		Zone - OLLEZY - No 3 ANNOIS. Labouring labour available for work. One Company Between Company Labelled at PITHON. One Company SOMMETTE - one Company ST SIMON. One battalion 6" K.R.R.C. and 60" T.M. Batt at CUGNY. Company Redoubts took B. Spitsbergen. Labour attack Pals and 8.S.P. 5 S.P. wire carried out, also strengthening redoubts & empty new wiring. Lock forwarded rapidly on last week; 20 cut pr-1st Sch 110 cut pr-2nd Sch	
	14th-20th		One company R.I.R. (entrenching Bn.) attached for work at battalion at CUGNY. Work continued as usual in Rear Zone Defences.	
	21st		Heavy enemy attack on front. Warning order received 18th Corps morning Battle Stations. Company ordered to man battle at St. SULPICE (near Ham). Spare transport & battery trans. ordered to VERCOURS.	
ST SULPICE	22nd		20.17 Sch move to front to Coll Bde at AUBIGNY to & return to front. Heraldic dug a line of posts on front of AUBIGNY & relieve of Bde to held them until infantry fell back & took over.	

WAR DIARY / INTELLIGENCE SUMMARY

Army Form C. 2118.

SHEET. No. A.   83rd Field Coy. R.E.

SECRET

Place	Date	Hour	Summary of Events and Information	Remarks and references to Appendices
	22"		Nos 1 & 3 Sections ordered to report to company at 11 p.m. for demolition work. Division ordered to relieve fighting troops & take up position in Rear Zone of Defences S. of SOMME CANAL between CANIZY and BETHENCOURT. Bridges over the Canal from CANIZY - EVOYENNES inclusive allotted to Company to demolish.	
	23"		At 6th Hour of 23rd infantry across Companies Rd. Bridges were reported to have been prepared for demolition under Corps arrangements. Preliminary work to establish demolition found to be entirely unsatisfactory; on bridges no circuit or testing leads, charges on 3 bridges far too small, & in case the main fuzes & bridges had been opened. His bridges not prepared at all. Fortunately as it turned out, we were not ordered have fuzes to blow & by 7.30 am 10 heavy trestle bridges had with one exception complete & satisfactory info made in time. (See Capt. Hurdate's substituted appendix "A") Company moved to ERCHEU & arrived at 10 p.m. to look for truck at BACANCOURT. Spare transport & hopping wagons ordered to CARREPUIS.	
BACANCOURT	24"		Information by Brigade that enemy had crossed Canal at CANIZY, Ordered off	

Army Form C. 2118.

WAR DIARY or INTELLIGENCE SUMMARY

SHEET 2 83rd Inf Bde R3. SECRET

(Erase heading not required.)

Place	Date	Hour	Summary of Events and Information	Remarks and references to Appendices
BACONCOURT	24"		At 8 am to move my company to a new line. Informed at 9.30 am by Brigade that the right flank was in the air and that enemy was advancing down main road from HAM towards HOMBLEUX. Ordered by Brigade to move my company to this flank, engage the enemy + establish defensive flank. Sent forward cyclists patrols and advanced guard company, less H.Q. & Transport, advanced in artillery formation. Reported by advanced guard about 10.30 am that they could not locate enemy, main body machine guns + right rifles on left flank, moved forward in extended order to establish a defensive flank on the high ground running N.E. + S.W. one mile E. of HOMBLEUX. Two sections on left — our centre + no 3 on right, no 2 Reserve. Collected wounded stragglers from 30th Division + a strong A+A of mixed units 12 K.R.R.C. and Artillery, made E of HOMBLEUX, left in touch about 1500 yds S.E. along the ridge, much to left in touch, and any troops on right. Situation reported to Bde at M.Ham ct. ? and any forces collected extended front to attack but situation on right flank dangerous.	

WAR DIARY or INTELLIGENCE SUMMARY

Army Form C. 2118.

SHEET III   B" Field by RE
             B 30th Divn
SECRET

Place	Date	Hour	Summary of Events and Information	Remarks and references to Appendices

During the forenoon repeated attempts of enemy to advance were held up by rifle fire and the assistance of one detn from B 30 "Divn.

Report that at 1.15 pm to 60 "Bde stating position on my left had become fairly [serious?] on my right flank, also requested further ammunition & machine gun.

Received report from Lt Poole 1.45 pm Enemy had pressed in charge of my right flank post, that he was the 4 Section sent up to reinforce right flank & ammunition urgently required. Reft, 200-300 nearer. La la attached & sent up also 2.30 pm. Report from Lt Poole, suffering heavy casualties & being outflanked by enemy in strength, enemy also moving in small bodies & concentrating in wood near GRECOURT. Two M.G.'s from holes hacking in company Shed to cover my right flank from HOMBLEUX & HAM and believed to into small wood near GRECOURT when enemy apparent concentrating.

3 pm. Report from Lt Poole ammunition running out, enemy forcing hard on right flank. Orders sent to Lt Poole to hold on at all costs.

3.30 pm. Artillery & determined enemy attack all along my front, losses from enemy machine gun & shrapnel fire heavy.

WAR DIARY or INTELLIGENCE SUMMARY

Army Form C. 2118.

Sheet IV

83rd Field Coy R.E.

SECRET

Place	Date	Hour	Summary of Events and Information	Remarks and references to Appendices

Right flank arm to be falling back on HOMBLEUX. I, who don't trust them on immediate left, as far as Railway embankment has withdrawn. Advise this withdrawal on HOMBLEUX from its right; heavy engaged with enemy at close quarters during withdrawal + suffered heavy casualties. Remain in HOMBLEUX to By Interment of Lyt-woulds in Ashby in line near from HOMBLEUX to By Interment of Lyt-woulds in Ashby 7 pm. Repaired to 60th Bn MG on BACUNCOURT CANAL LINE - to BILLANCOURT. Ordered by CRE to move to NESLE without delay. Enemy to advance of 2" motorway to form 3 sections at 12 mm No. 1 Section abutter in Nos. 2, 3 + 4. Guided by CRE 6 more Company from his Station to CREMERY forthwith, recomm + commence work on new line RETHONVILLERS - CRESNY - along this line + by exavating old trenches leave a good strong line made + prev'sly wired by infantry by midnight. Span handful + company taking MM. from CREMERY 15 fools they Manchesters away to MANCHEST-EN-SANTERRE.

RETHONVILLERS "25"

WAR DIARY or INTELLIGENCE SUMMARY

Army Form C. 2118.

SHEET V

93rd Field Coy R.E.

SECRET

Place	Date	Hour	Summary of Events and Information	Remarks and references to Appendices
HANGEST-EN-SANTERRE	26th		Company ordered to join 60th Bn. front concentrating at ROYE at 6.30 am & march to QUESNEL.	
	27th		Relieved by C.R.E. to duty that 18 parks E. of HANGEST-EN-SANTERRE, refusing its right flank towards PLESSIER. – 18 parks ready by Company. Spare transport sent to DOMART-SUR-LA-LUCE.	
DOMART-SUR-LUCE	28th		Company ordered to conceal hole at DOMART in wood S.E. of village. Transport moved to BOVES.	
	29th		Company ordered to construct two 18 parks along MOREUIL-DEMUIN Rd from AMIENS-ROYE ROAD running to in rear of DEMUIN & turning to approach march along the river LUCE. 18 parks ready 7pm. Stand down 10pm.	
BOVES	30th		Company ordered to move to battle at BOVES. 18 parks ready 5 Company running NE & SW through road junction South, 85 in BOIS de GENIÈRES. 12 parks ready. Company transport rejoined Company at BOVES.	
	31st		Company in battle at BOVES. Battle Casualties for march however.	

	Killed	Wounded	missing, wounds, Strong
		2	3
	1 Off. 21 O.R.		1
			Influence Killed wounds

Coy Strength end of march. 7 Off. 174 O.R.

2449 Wt. W14957/M90 750,000 1/16 J.B.C. & A. Forms/C.2118/12.

O.C. 83rd F(d Coy R.E.   6.4.18

REPORT
ON DEMOLITION OF BRIDGES AT OFFOY.

On night 21.3.18 — 22.3.18 I was ordered by you to demolish bridges at OFFOY which were reported to have been completely prepared for demolition by 18th Corps.

On arrival at site at 2.0 am. I found that Bridges A & C only had been prepared and on testing the circuits I found that the leads on bridge A had been cut (apparently not accidentally) and that one of the electric detonators had been broken.

In addition to this the centre girder of the bridge at

a on sketch had been completely ignored by whoever prepared the bridge for demolition.

2

Time would not permit of altering the laying of the charges as the centre girder was very difficult of access.

I destroyed the centre girder after blowing the other charges by an extra charge laid by hand & actuated by time fuse.

I had only 4 hours to lay charges for the other 3 bridges and the dam at E and also to lay the leads &c to Bridge A.

I laid charges on subsidiary bridge at B (32 slabs) & the dam at E (80 slabs) and demolished these beforehand about 5.0 a.m.

I charged the trestle Bridge at D with 32 slabs on the trestle & 16 slabs on the road bearers. and the heavy wooden bridge at F with 48 slabs in 3 charges over the main bearers which were tree trunks

3

About 7.0 a.m. on Col. Moon reporting that all his battalion were over the bridges, I blew A, C, D & F bridges in succession.

Complete gaps were produced in every case except A & C bridges which had been prepared by 18th Corps.

These two I finished off by extra charges laid by hand afterwards.

R M Huddart
Capt. R.E.
83rd Fd Coy R.E.

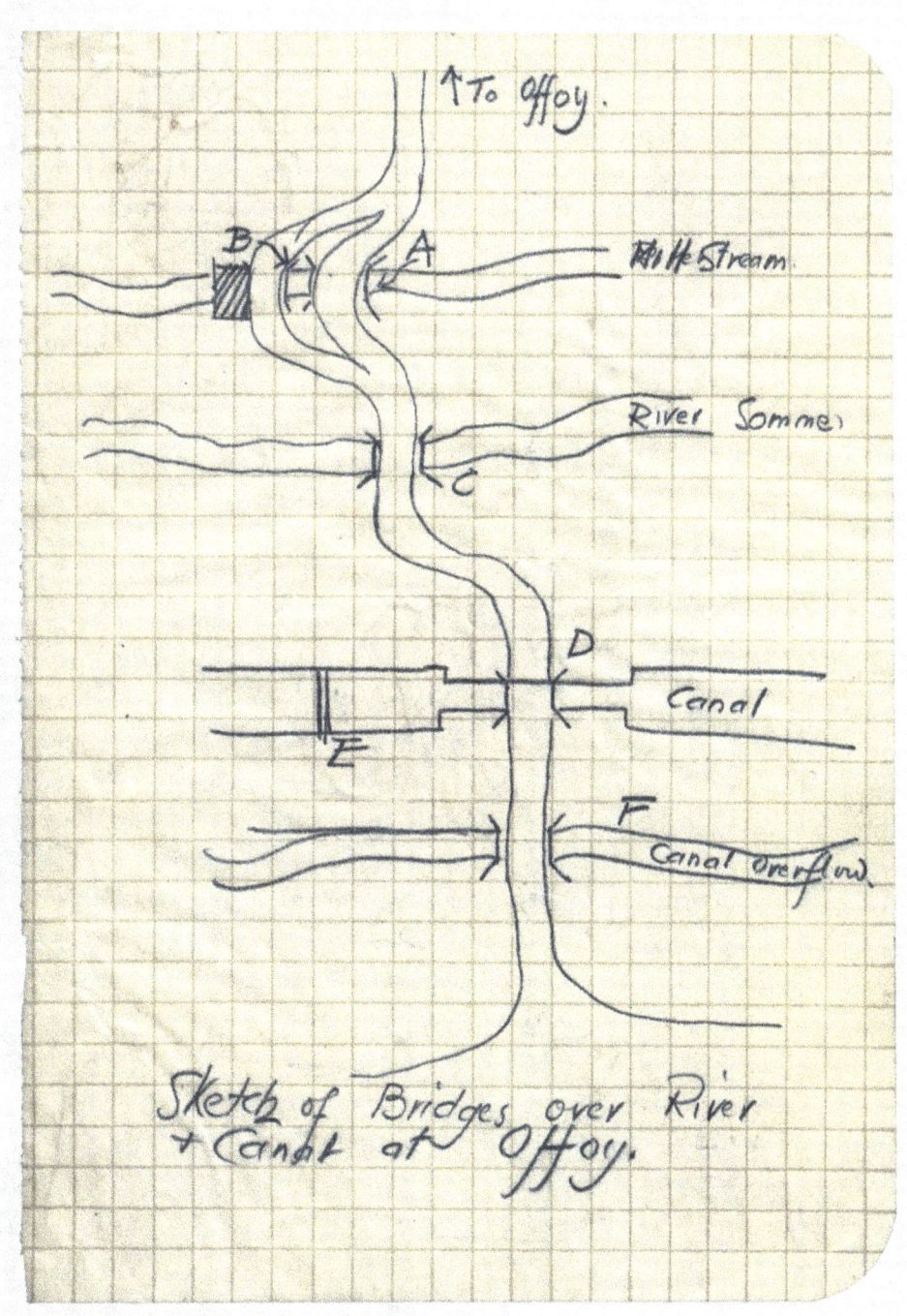

SECRET

WAR DIARY
INTELLIGENCE SUMMARY
(Erase heading not required.)

83rd Field Coy. R.E.

Army Form C. 2118.

Vol 34

Place	Date	Hour	Summary of Events and Information	Remarks and references to Appendices
BOVES. Shot AMIENS.	31st March		Coys. complete at BOVES. Battalion HQ. infantry and I tank to their sup on 30 mts. in front of BOIS de SENTELET.	
	1st April		Proceeded reviewing by lorry to QUEVAUVILLERS. Coys. marched to billets at PRESNOY-au-VAL.	
	2nd "		Clean up and rest at PRESNOY.	
	3rd "		Company marched to billets at ST AUBIN-MONTENOY.	
	4-7 "		" " "	
	8 "		Infantry training	
	9 "		" "	
	10 "		Company marched to BROCOURT	
	12 "		" " BAIRNAST.	
			" " VISE.	
			" " BEAUCHAMPS.	
BEAUCHAMPS. Shot ABBEVILLE.	13'-14		Carried on refuge by trained manoeuvring	
	15 "		Proceeded for two days John to trains. 83 Coy. + details cart-marched to entrain at EU. Remainder of transport moved by road to unite to FIRST ARMY area.	
	18 "		Entrained at EU for TURQUES. Transport to billets at CAUCHIN-LE-GAL.	
	19 "		Remainder Railway transport to road agreed company.	
	20 "			
CAUCHIN- LE-GAL Shot LENS.M.	21st-30 "		Following on the programme attached. Strength of Coy. 7 Off. 204 O.R. O. Dietrichs + 3.46 O.R. paid Coy. Lt McGrath transferred 6th "2" Coy and 2nd in command 25th Field Coy. Lt Potter. Canadian Military transferred.	

Training Programme. 3rd Week. Ending 5th Aug.   83rd Field Reg RA.

DAY	SESSION	7.30-8.30am	8.30-9.30 am	9.30-10.30am	10.30-11.30am	11.30-12.30pm	6/...
1st DAY MON	No 1	Squad Drill. Bayonet fighting.	Huskety training. Individual field in training.	Knowledge tanks.	Elementary anti-tank drill.	Knowledge tanks. Bayonet fighting.	
	No 2		Enroute to Gym. Mecm. 2 Co				
	No 3	Bren + Sten Drill	Gas Drill	Instruction	Anti-Gas + tank drill. Physical training + bayonet fighting.		
	No 4		Range Firing.	Gunnery Drill + instructions / anti-tank 100yds	Vigorous out thorough kapok + relaxing out. looking forward.		
2nd DAY TUES	No 1	Section Drill	"	Anti-tank	Drill + training.	Firing.	
	No 2		Range firing			Bayonet fighting. Recreational training.	
	No 3	Section route march (compulsory). Sleep in defence of HOUSEKEEP.					
	No 4		Gunnery Gym. Shoots etc.				
3rd DAY WED	No 1	Company Drill	Lecture in Mapreading.	Instruction in compass.	Firing.	Night Scheme compass bch + laying out track	
	No 2	"	"	Range training	Map reading.	" "	
	No 3	"	Firemaking. Rationing/ Cooking camp.	"	Not sleeping on compass bch.	Anti-Tank approaches + field setup.	
	No 4	"	Physical training + bayonet fighting	Firing (all arms compass bch)	(Wing ? Softness (?chaps)	Return to barrack Make Toilet	Setting out, hut inspection etc.

Training General. Issued (with House Leaflet) P.30a, 6.9.
Rifle Range. Nos 6.6.F.6.
Field looks & Bayfing. P.3Ed. L.2.

Training Programme 3rd Week.   83rd Field Coy R.E.

Day	Sunday 5th May			
	6:30 – 8:30	9:30 – 10:30 am	10:30 – 11:30 am	11:30 – 12:30 pm	afternoon
7.1	Company Drill.		Field books.	M.E. Vol I, Secs. 3+4 Part V. para 176.	Preparing equipment

1st Day 2nd   " "   Section Signs. Saddle Bridge.   Night School
3rd   Gas Drill.   Section training. Rogue's march.   Ryot School
                Physical training. Latrine   setting trap. Preparation of laying out Pickets
  4   Physical training. Latrine   Reading.   Manual knowledge
                 Bayonet fighting.   construction.   map reading.
                 Field books. – Use of Haversack, Mines & Spirals. Shooting training apparatus diagrams.

  1   Gas Drill
  2   Section Route march. Scheme: Defence of BERGIN.
5th Day   complete with transport.
  3   Sereko. Signs. Suva. Lion Bridge.
  4   Section Route march. Scheme. Sitting Defence of HOUVELM.
                 complete with transport.

  1   Section Route march. Scheme. Defence of BERGIN.
6th Day 2   Section Drill.   Gas Drill   Mining.
  3   Bay's drenin. Application & repair of gas gas.
  4   Gas Drill   Bayonet fighting. Lewis gun & Sports + football
                                             testing.

Note:- Sunday Drill. Bayonet Drill. Rating School. Sunny Drill
       Sunday: Kit inspection. Church Parade. Sports.

                                                   J Shrapnel
                                                   Major R.E.
                                                   83rd Field Coy R.E.

Training Programme, 2nd Week — 83rd Ft Coy R.E.

Day	Section	8.30 to 9.30 am	9.30 to 10.30 am	10.30 to 11.30 am	11.30 am to 12.30 pm	Afternoon
1st Day	No. 1	Squad Drill	Musketry – aiming & rapid loading	Lecture on Map reading	Demolition Exam	Cleaning Wagons & rifles
	No. 2	ditto		Knots & lashings	Lecture on tokar	ditto
	No. 3	ditto	Gas Drill	Musketry aiming & rapid loading	Physical training & bayonet fighting	ditto
	No. 4	ditto	Gas Drill	Musketry triangle of Error	Lecture in placing of charges	ditto
2nd Day	No. 1			Pontooning		
	No. 2			Wiring		
	No. 3	Squad Drill	Lecture on Sanitation, Health & care of feet		Lecture on schedules, how carried & distribution of the same during Field Musketry	Knots & lashings, Blocks & tackle, Physical training & bayonet fighting
	No. 4	ditto	Rapid loading & snapping at safe triangle of Error	Bayonet fighting		Knots & lashings, Blocks & tackle, Recreational training
3rd Day	No. 1	ditto	Musketry snap shooting & rapid fire	Visual training	Knots & lashings, Blocks & tackle	Map reading, Reconnaissance
	No. 2	ditto	Gas Drill	Lecture on Musketry	Triangle of Error during Rapid loading	Demolition Lecture
	No. 3			Pontooning		Recreational Training & bayonet fighting
	No. 4			Pontooning		

Training Programme 2nd week　　　　　83rd Field Coy R.E.

Section	8.30 to 9.30 am	9.30 to 10.30 am	10.30 to 11.30 am	11.30 to 12.30 pm	Afternoon
No. 1	Squad Drill		Derricks, Gyns, Shears.		Musketry firing positions rapid loading Taking Cover
No. 2	ditto	Demolition Scheme			Map reading pointing out objects from hill. Setting map company marching
4th Day No. 3	ditto	Gas Drill	Musketry Triangle of Error using fire control	Physical training	Compass marching
No. 4	ditto	Explosives & Demolitions			Wiring
No. 1	ditto		Derricks Gyns Shears etc		(Derricks Retaind)
No. 2	ditto	Musketry Triangle of Error fire discipline	Wiring		Bayonet fighting. Physical Training
5th Day No. 3	ditto	Musketry fire discipline Control		Making Range	Range firing grouping Application & rapid fire
No. 4	ditto	Gas Drill	Scheme lecture on Defence of Village		ditto
No. 1	ditto	Gas Drill	Musketry use of Taking Cover firing positions	Visual Training	
No. 2	ditto	Derricks, Gyns, Shears etc.			(Derricks Retaind)
6th Day No. 3	ditto	Range firing			100 yds jumping with Bayonet 100 " " without Bayonet
No. 4	ditto	Gas Drill	Wiring		Physical Training & Bayonet fighting

2 p.m. Senior N.C.O. Instruction & Cookers

Army Form C. 2118.

83rd FIELD COMPANY, R.E.
No. 0456
Date

WC 35

WAR DIARY or INTELLIGENCE SUMMARY
(Erase heading not required.)

Place	Date	Hour	Summary of Events and Information	Remarks and references to Appendices
GAUCHIN-LEGAL. CARENCY- SOUCHEZ Rd X 17 b 4.2	1917 MAY 1st		Training at Gauchin - Legal.	
	2nd		Company moves to new area nr Souchez & relieve 7th Canadian Inf. Bde Fd Coy taking over right of Div. Sector by 60th Bde. Boundary LM 25d 8.9.	
	3rd		Boundary R T2d 6.0. 91st Inf. Bde on left. Trench System recconaitred.	
			Forward Billets established at IRISH SUPPORT.	
			Work consists of Tunnelled Dug outs	
	4th		No 4 Section move to Forward Billets & take over left subsector	
	5th		" 2 " " " " " right "	
	6th		" 3 " " " Intermediate & in Brown Line S10d 8.6 & take over wiring & firestepping.	
	7th, 8th, 9th		Work normal.	
	10th		No 1 Section relieved No 4 who carry on training & back work at Horse lines	
	11th, 12th		Work normal. LE Dieterichs commences work on "special" light railway siding	
	13th		No 2 Section under Lt Dieterichs at TQ b 66, H 32d 2.5, H 25 6.3.6.	
	16th, 17th		Work normal.	
	18th		Relieved of forward work except special L.R. line, by 96th Fld Coy.	
			Nos 1, 2 & 3 Section return to Horse lines	
	19th		Kit inspection &c.	
	20th		Training. Musketry on range, Drill, Rifle Exercises.	
	21st		Training. Maintenance of special L.R. line	
	22		" " " " "	

WAR DIARY
or
INTELLIGENCE SUMMARY

Army Form C. 2118.

Place	Date MAY	Hour	Summary of Events and Information	Remarks and references to Appendices
CARENCY – SOUCHEZ RD. X 11.4.2.	23rd		Training. Zero hour gas attack. 17.0 min. Lt. Dietrich with 3 N.C.O.s + details from No. A Section went up to repair + maintain the new KINGSTON, AVION + DORIS line in connexion with the attack. The line were successfully repaired + maintained during the whole of the operation + the gas cylinders successfully employed on the new line. 75 trucks were pushed up on each line, each containing 21 cylinders. The cylinders were meantime discharged between 3.0 + 3.0 am by Electric detonators which opened a sealed tube. All the trucks were got away again with the help of this open except 35 on the KINGSTON line which was blocked near ADEPT by a derailment. The D.L.I. Pushing party were in too great a hurry + a column of the trucks was derailed subsequently. One occurred detailing attack. They succeed to clear time by the remain of 50 slightly passed keeping at bay gas leaking from cylinders.	
	24th		Training + wetting huts. Physical drill, bayonet fighting, Musketry or range. Gas danger hut at ANGERS. Stretcher + Baths at CARENCY.	
	25th		Training	
	26th		Work normal. Stretcher bearer class started under Capt TOWNSHEND	
	27th		Baths. No 2 Section training. M+S 1+4 relieve 96th Fd. Coy in the forward area. Horse lines shifted.	
	28th			
	29th		Baths at CARENCY finished. Two Nissen huts taken down. One carried to LENS JUNCTION. To D.W. H.Q. Horse lines shifted.	

Army Form C. 2118.

WAR DIARY
or
INTELLIGENCE SUMMARY
(Erase heading not required.)

Instructions regarding War Diaries and Intelligence Summaries are contained in F.S. Regs., Part II. and the Staff Manual respectively. Title Pages will be prepared in manuscript.

Place	Date MAY	Hour	Summary of Events and Information	Remarks and references to Appendices
CARENCY SOUCHEZ RD. X17 b 4.2	30th		No 4 Section working on GAS (Hanging Rm) + Erecting Horse hut at Div. H-Q. During the month:- 2 Bdr. to Battalion trained in using also Bde when trained in trench digging + Lectures. M.S. L. 1. — Reinforcements = 11 O.R. from base. Casualties = 1 " " wounded at duty. Honours & Awards. Major T.W. MASSIE M.C. — bar. Lt. F.A. POOLE — Military Cross 46205 Gy JOYCE) Military Medal. 56957 Cpl. GIBSON) Company Strength at end of Month. 7 Officers. 209 O.R. RM Stewart Capt R.E. O/C. 83rd Field Co. R.E.	

WAR DIARY or INTELLIGENCE SUMMARY

Army Form C. 2118.
8 3 79 Cay R2

Place	Date	Hour	Summary of Events and Information	Remarks and references to Appendices
CARENCY- SOUCHEZ Rd. X17/6 4.2	JUNE 1st		Camp Normal. Work Normal.	
	2nd		A.D.S. CYRIL TR. started. Splinter proof shelters in camp started.	
	3rd		Camp & trail shelled during morning. Moved Hme line temporarily + men killed.	
	4th		Camp shelled. Work normal. Leave of men. about 2 per Division.	
	5th		4.0 a.m. had orders to man battle stations (practice). Sections found & manned to usual station in error. Vide Appendix 4. (Spent sent to R.E. Raid made by 60th Bde on night of 4th-5th. 1 N.C.O. & 3 sapper went out with the party but infantry did not provide sufficient guides to men to carry the guncotton + those guides detailed to the sapper lost touch with the Raid party. The infantry failed in their objectives so that in any case the sapper would not have been able to destroy the dugout or way the intention. Sapper GOUGH wounded. On the attention of the 5th the 2 section back & mounted branch were inspected by G.O.C. Division at 5.0 p.m.	
	6th		No 2 & 3 sections relieve no 1-4 forward. Work continuing & normal.	
	7th		More men & huns back into camp a skilling ha cards. Start a day course of special training for N.C.O.s of No 1+4 sections. Lecture and examination taken every evening by officers. These 2 sections showed up to the line has necessary & imperative good training particularly for the N.C.O.'s. (Batn. Garrison CARENCY status).	
	8th 9th 10th 11th		No 3 on left employed m Baby shelters. No 4 on right mainly on Dugout. No 4 working m Dugouts in LORRETTE area. Work normal.	
	12th 13th		Lt Dietrich A. RFA & Q.	
	14th		No 1 Section start at SOUCHEZ. No 3 section start on Dugouts at S16 6 14 for numbers twelve mantle huts tracet at ST NAZAIRE	Mildren Capt

Army Form C. 2118.

WAR DIARY
or
INTELLIGENCE SUMMARY

(Erase heading not required.)

Instructions regarding War Diaries and Intelligence Summaries are contained in F. S. Regs., Part II. and the Staff Manual respectively. Title Pages will be prepared in manuscript.

Place	Date	Hour	Summary of Events and Information	Remarks and references to Appendices
CARENCY-SOUCHEZ Rd. X17b 4.2	JUNE 15th		No change.	
	16th		Relieved in Forward area by 96th Fld Coy. Infantry at Dumps & relieved & brought back. C.R.E. & A.A. & Q.M.G. go on leave. Major Mann goes to Div.H.S.	
	17th		Nos 2 & 3 section training. No 1 section moving camp to St NAZAIRE ST NAZAIRE 24/CRE	
	18th		No 4 section on Gunpits at X 6c + R34 d Battery Nos 2 & 3	
	19th		No change.	
	20th 21st 22nd 23rd		Disinfestor started by No 4 section at CARENCY Work + training normal Baths.	
	24th 25th		Complete moving camp to St NAZAIRE	
			Start moving COLUMBIA CAMP to ABLAIN ST NAZAIRE. Take over Forward work from 96th Fld Coy. Work chiefly new sit + R.F.A. Bde H.Q. + Coy + platoon accommodation in SIDNEY - BADDECK - BLUENOSE area necessitated by change in the disposition.	
	26th 27 28 29 30th		Camp shifting to 96th in back area handed over. Work normal. No 4 still working on gunpits.	

REINFORCEMENTS from BASE during month   9 O.R.S.
CASUALTIES Wounded at duty   3
HONOURS & AWARDS   50963 C.S.M. CHAPMAN S. } Meritorious Service Medal.
52506 Sergt. DICKSON J. }

COMPANY STRENGTH at end of Month. 7 officers 212 O.R.S.

R.M Townshend
4/Lt. 83rd Fld Coy R.E.

88rd FIELD COMPANY, R.E.
No. D 686
Date 30.6.16

WAR DIARY
or
INTELLIGENCE SUMMARY

Army Form C. 2118.

83 70 Coy RE

Place	Date	Hour	Summary of Events and Information	Remarks and references to Appendices
MALON CAMP CARENCY- SOUCHEZ Rd X17b4.2	JULY 1st		Nos 2 & 3 Sections employed in forward area on deep dugouts, protecting shelters. No 1 Patrolling, maintaining back line &c. Camp, gunpits in rear position & accommodation for gun crews.	
	5th		No 1 MG section to back area. Included (turned over) by 2 & 3. Similar work continued.	
	14th		Alteration of system of into company reliefs. Each Coy. instd of red arrangement to a definite sector & is self relieving. 84th & 96th have half of Lift. sector each & Batt. work whole if. Pte. Rife continuing. Billets take our gunpits in sector.	
	15th		Nos 2 & 3 sections return to back then turn take over etc (tours) back area from 1 & 2 sections who in their BC work which is still chiefly dugouts in this sector carried out a raid in Rly Embankment at N 27 c 5.6. CH. Roberts & Sapper went out with the Raiding party of 4 platoons & Rev again to his sappers to advance first under a smoke cloud and blow 2 gaps in the wire. As soon as the torpedoes went off the infantry went to rush the gaps & the enemy trench doing what damage they could. At zero plus 15 min. stood watching what persons they could, but unfortunately the artillery were to fire on certain selected targets but unfortunately circumstances were very adverse. The smoke cloud formed by burning smoke candles in the authority lin. was supposed to come down at zero — 5. It failed to reach any state march objective and at zero the sappers had to crawl forward without it & place the torpedoes.	

at 12—23

WAR DIARY
or
INTELLIGENCE SUMMARY

Army Form C. 2118.

Place	Date	Hour	Summary of Events and Information	Remarks and references to Appendices
MALON CAMP	JULY 22-23		"At zero + 5 one torpedo was placed. The other could not be placed owing to the sudden appearance of an enemy patrol on the opposite side of the wire. It was decided therefore to fire one only in the one in place, which was accordingly done at ZERO + 15 min. + the infantry dashed thro' the gap in fine style in about 15 seconds. This infim effort unfortunately reported from being ruined by an other raid, on the immediate left (which took place on our own shell stopping short of enemy's trench) casualties went from one area MOS 1 + 4 being one set of gaspits in the track area owr the new set of gaspits with 92R. Poultry 20t out was being writing intrebash team which was sent over very very worn away but theseation learn."	
	31.		REINFORCEMENTS FROM BASE during month. 3. CASUALTIES wounded at duty nil HONOURS & AWARDS nil 6 off. 212 O.R.s COMPANY STRENGTH at end of month	

Phillsdeyeut
Captain
for O.C. 63rd Field Co.

SECRET WAR DIARY 83rd Field Coy RE Army Form C. 2118.
or
INTELLIGENCE SUMMARY
(Erase heading not required.)

Place	Date	Hour	Summary of Events and Information	Remarks and references to Appendices
LA FOLIE WOOD. S23C.4.4.	1st Aug		Coy Strength 6 Offs. 212 O.R. Nos 1 & 3 Sections employed on forward work. Handy dug outs - Further had Phillies & drainage of huts. System. No 1 & 4 Sections employed on back area work. Dug outs & camp work.	VIII 38
	4th		No 1 & 4 Sections moved to forward billets near GIVENCHY and took on work in forward area relieving No 2 & 3 Sections who moved to Hut Lines & took on back work.	
	6th		L/Cpl Mitchell and Spr Dickinson accompanied raiding party 9/12 KRRC. Bangalore Torpedoes were placed in wire but blown out by keep fire from an Enemy M.G. Sapper Bailey, sapper bally [?] killed. A second attempt to place more Torpedoes was similarly foiled.	
			No 2 & 3 Sections relieved No 1 & 4 & took on forward area. No 1 & 4 took on back area work.	
	12th		Coy Bn moved to Late Van Bac Huts on night (MERICOURT SECTOR) advance parties out to take over 157th Field Coy 8th Divn. Work made [?] took in LA's. MERICOURT SECTOR work of 1st Field Coy. No particularly urgent work in Line & schedule to carry on with as before stuff.	
	13th		No 1 Section from D/M 158/74 F.O.R.	
	19th		Congratulations of Army & Divisn received on forms stating [?]	

SECRET WAR DIARY 83rd Field Coy R.E.
          or
SHEET II INTELLIGENCE SUMMARY

Army Form C. 2118.

(Erase heading not required.)

Place	Date	Hour	Summary of Events and Information	Remarks and references to Appendices
D'ng	21 Aug		R'Cpt Mitchell awarded Military Medal for following deed of Infantry 6" Relieved of work in AVION SECTOR by 5th Field Coy. No 1 & 4 Sections moved to new billet at S.13.C.4.4. & commenced work in MERICOURT SECTOR. Making Bdes. O.P. Bdr. Visual Sta. & Tunnel Dugouts. Supervising Staff of two Trenches, overhauling & relaying Plank Paths in VIMY RIDGE & UPPER & BROWN No 2 & 3 Sections moved to Bois Ballot etc. Sunspots, fillers for Bois Ballot etc. Company HQ, No 2 Pnrs in Corps Horse Show event. Took cart + train complete under mounted HQs. This team won 1st Prize in Div R.E. Show in Similar Class. Reinforcements during month — 1 Officer B.O.R. Awards " " — 1 Infantry Medal Casualties " " — 1 O.R. wounded at duty Cg Strength 7 Offr. 214 O.R.	LINE.

M Barnard Capt R.E.
O.C. 83rd Field Coy R.E.

SECRET

83rd Field Coy. R.E.

Army Form C. 2118.

WAR DIARY
or
INTELLIGENCE SUMMARY.
(Erase heading not required.)

Instructions regarding War Diaries and Intelligence Summaries are contained in F. S. Regs., Part II. and the Staff Manual respectively. Title pages will be prepared in manuscript.

Place	Date	Hour	Summary of Events and Information	Remarks and references to Appendices
MALON CAMP near SOUCHEZ T.17.6.4.2.	6/9/17 1st		Coy Strength 7 Offs 214 O.R. No 1 & 4 Sections employed on Forward Works in "B" area. Camouflaging lines - curves roads, making Lionel dugouts. Digging & wiring Shelter pits on forward slope of VIMY RIDGE. Draining, levelling trenches. General improvement of Infantry work. No 2 & 3 Sections relieve No 1 & 4 sections for forward work - later one work in Back area, Sec. Wag + repair of Camps, lamp drainage, Allin for Divl Baths etc. Tramway.	
	3rd			
	15th		No 1 & 4 Sects relieve No 2 & 3 Sections of work in forward area who take over Back work + training.	
	19/20		Raid by 13th KRRC on enemy trenches E. of HULL ROAD MERICOURT SECTOR. Two Sappers / No 2 Sect detailed to examine out come by Bangalore Lopedo. Raid very successful. 1 prisoner taken. Spr Lully's work lightly commended by O/C of Raiding Party.	
	27th		No 2 & 3 Section took over forward work from No 1 & 4 Section. Reinforcements during month, 4 O.R. 1 OR wounded.	Coy Strength 7 Offs 30/9/17. 7 Offs 206 O.R's

J. Rennie Capt A
83 Field Coy RE

1st Div

1st Bde & Units

October 1918

SECRET

WAR DIARY or INTELLIGENCE SUMMARY

Army Form C. 2118.

63rd Field Coy. R.E.

Place	Date	Hour	Summary of Events and Information	Remarks and references to Appendices
LA FOLIE WOOD. S 23 C.4A	Oct. 1st		No's 2 & 3 Sections working on Dugouts for new Batt. H.Q. & camouflaging LENS ARRAS Rd. & maintenance of tracks. Remaining Sections working on camp & drainage in back area.	
	3rd		Training. Owing to signs of enemy withdrawal the company ordered to concentrate at new (unnamed) village at T26 a 3.8 on NEW BRUNSWICK ROAD W. of ACHEVILLE. Arrived there 1700. Started work on repair of NEW BRUNSWICK & LENS ARRAS Roads. 110 Infantry attacked this m.g. Road was damaged by horse transport to that extn. Work held up (owing to that) owing to failure of main attack on ACHEVILLE.	
	4th 5th		Continued repair of roads in day & night shifts. Relieved at night in the line by 70 Field Coy. 12th Div. at 12.30. Dismounted personnel move by lorry to ESTREE CAUCHIE. Transport moved by road.	
ESTREE CAUCHIE.	6th 7th		Resting & Cleaning up.	
	8th 21st 24th 23rd		Begin training. Light Bridge construction. Rough Wood Trestle Bridge training. (Firing in CAUCOURT Range.) Training, & fastening Inter Section training competition.	
	25th 26th		Capt. T.W.R. HAYCROFT arrived from 39th Divn to take over command from Major I.W. MASSIE, M.C. appointed C.R.E. 71st Div. Officers & Senior N.C.O.s to Army Bridging School all day. General parade in marching order, Cleaning & overhauling Wagons	

Army Form C. 2118.

WAR DIARY
or
INTELLIGENCE SUMMARY.
(Erase heading not required.)

Instructions regarding War Diaries and Intelligence Summaries are contained in F. S. Regs., Part II. and the Staff Manual respectively. Title pages will be prepared in manuscript.

Place	Date	Hour	Summary of Events and Information	Remarks and references to Appendices
ESTREE-CAUCHIE	17th 18th 29th 30th		Baths. Recreational Training. Training in Platoon holidays. 1 section firing on range. Training & football match. Coy. entrained at TINQUES at 6.00 + moved by rail to FREMI COURT + thence to billets in CAMBRAI — Dismounted lorries + transport & Cyclists by road	
CAMBRAI	31st		Rest during moving transport & cleaning up in afternoon. Reinforcements during month " Officers " O.R's " nil " 7 206 Coy. strength at beginning of month " 7 201	

Casualties

Ruttledge Captn.
O.C. 8th Fusiliers

Ref LENS 11 1/10,000   SECRET   WAR DIARY or INTELLIGENCE SUMMARY.   83rd Field Co. R.E.   Army Form C. 2118.

Place	Date	Hour	Summary of Events and Information	Remarks and references to Appendices
FAMECHON (LENS 11 5F.65.72)	Dec 2nd	7-	No 1 Sec. continued work for 61st Bde. at VAYC. HELLZ camp (5F.7.1.) No 4 Sec. moved to MEESER (5G.2.5.) to work in 60th Bde. area — repairing and building barns, repairing baths & erecting new huttings for accommodation & recreation.	
	7th	7-	No 2 Sec. moved to POMMIER (4H.2.2.) To work for 20th Div. S.C. - repairing & building barns, erecting cookhouses & standings for 800 horses	
	8th		No 3 Sec. moved to BUS (5G.5.2.) To erect 12 Nissen huts for 12th R.B.	
	13th		No 3 Sec. completed work at BUS & moved to AUTHIE (5F.9.4.) to work for 6th K.S.L.I. — erecting new huttings for billets, dining rooms & recreation.	
	23rd		No 2 Sec. completed all work at POMMIER. All 4 Secs. returned to Co. H.Q. for Xmas.	
	25th 27th		Xmas leave	
	27th to 31st		Nos 1, 3 & 4 Secs returned to detached billets & continued work. All work continued.	

Reinforcements during month   Officers Nil   O.R.s 1
Casualties   Nil   Nil
Co. Strength beginning of month   7   205
Co. Strength end of month   7   [?]

Tepman(?)
Capt.
O.C. 83 Fd Co RE

SECRET
Army Form C. 2118.

WAR DIARY
or
INTELLIGENCE SUMMARY.

83rd FIELD COY RE

(Erase heading not required.)

Instructions regarding War Diaries and Intelligence Summaries are contained in F.S. Regs., Part II. and the Staff Manual respectively. Title pages will be prepared in manuscript.

Place	Date	Hour	Summary of Events and Information	Remarks and references to Appendices
FAMECHON			No 1 Section continuing work for 6th Bde at Vadencourt Camp (S8.U)	
			No 2 " work at FAMECHON Sec. 1.57.d.10.2.4. Bens & Repairs to Bldgs Mule Lines etc W Vauvillers	
			No 3 " continued to get Butments & Cribs ready for Timber on Bridge over the River	
			Doing & bridge sites (Berteaucourt) & got equipment ready for Bridging work. Repair of WAGON on	
			WAY & Crossings Refair of Bldgs Roads Bus arrived 12.15	
			W 1 Sect Completed work at Aux Representation Bldgs	
			W 2 " " Manure Pits Timbering Trenches & Dugouts Barracks & Offices	
			W 3 " Manure & Fruits, Water & Timber ST KEYSE	
			W 4 " and Completed work at Mc Gibbon ST KYSE	
			Lo 1 " (R1) Lye work of work instalation at Vauvillers	
			Lo 2 " (R2) Lye work repairs at E.C.Cottages & W.C.Cottages	
			Lo 3 " (R3) Lye work for 2 Offrs & 4 mens baths	
			Large M.T. shelter finished & ready for use. 12 mule Shelters Completed at Sonaipt	
			TOTALS Several Standard Huts and 6 Bund.	
			B.4. Loton Reinforcement arrived from base	
				Officers 2
				NCO's 17
			Completed shelter for funds	197
			Continued repairs & repairs & to Roads	1
				M.T. 2
				R.E. 4
				171
				180

REF LENS 11. 1/40000.   SECRET   WAR DIARY   or   INTELLIGENCE SUMMARY.   83RD FIELD COY. R.E.   Army Form C. 2118.

(Erase heading not required)

Instructions regarding War Diaries and Intelligence Summaries are contained in F.S. Regs., Part II. and the Staff Manual respectively. Title pages will be prepared in manuscript.

Place	Date	Hour	Summary of Events and Information	Remarks and references to Appendices
FAMECHON. LENS 11. (SF.65.72)	FEBY 1st		Nos 3 & 4 Secn continued Work at FlUTHIE (SF.9.4) Work on Thenlin. Engine House. Two kitchen Box Huts for Attels.	
	11th		Work commenced at BUS (SG.52) Erecting Cattle Shelter for M.Bouthor (Reclamation) Repair to MAIRIE	
	15th		Work at FAMECHON. Erecting Company Camp, Horse kitchen, 3 kitchen Box Hut & Cookhouse. Reclamation Work COUIN (S.G.33.65) Repair to Well. Buddle & Coll.	
	22nd		R.E. War Memorial. Saturieled by Company (two coats) £15.15. Cattle shell for M.Bouthor. BUS Completed.	
	24th		Repair to House	
	27th		Reclaimation Work COUIN. (S.6.40.58)	
			Reinforcements during Month. Casualties. Coy Strength beginning of Month. Coy Strength at end of Month.	Officers. O.R. Nil. Nil. Nil. Nil. 4. 150. 4. 118.

REF LENS 11.10000.
10 PW
Army Form C. 2118.

83RD FIELD Co RE

WAR DIARY
or
INTELLIGENCE SUMMARY.
(Erase heading not required)

Place	Date	Hour	Summary of Events and Information	Remarks and references to Appendices
FAMECHON LENS 11. (S.F 65:72)	MARCH 1.		Section continues work at BUS (5G 5.2) Repair to MAIRIE (Reclamation Work)	
	2a.		Work on MAIRIE completed	
	4.		Reclamation Work COIN (5G 3865) Repairs to Well (completed)	
			" (5G 40.38) Repair to Horse Reserve (completed)	
	18.			
	6.		Work at FAMECHON. Erecting Company Camp. (completed)	
	7.		Capt. R.H. Hodgson assumed command of Coy.	
	14.		" " " handed over	
				Officers OR
			Reinforcements during Month	N.L. N.L.
			Casualties	N.L. N.L.
				4. 118.
			Coy strength beginning of month	5. 119.
			Coy strength at end of month	

WAR DIARY or **INTELLIGENCE SUMMARY.**
(Erase heading not required.)

83RD FIELD. COY. R.E. Army Form C. 2118.

APRIL 1919

V/R 46

Place	Date	Hour	Summary of Events and Information	Remarks and references to Appendices
FAMECHON LENS 11 (5F 65.72)	APRIL 1919 1st		Cadre of Company awaiting orders for B[ ] proceed	
	1/10		for Demathegothin. Vehicles parked at :-	
	30th		MONDICOURT.	
	7th		LIEUT A McHAY proceeded to R.T. Coy. R.S. for duty as adjt R.S. a sub area in clearing up Army S.T.	
			CAPT R.H. HODGSON again assuming command of Company	
	30th		LIEUT H.M. GENOCHIO transferred to 84 TH FIELD COY. R.E.	
			HEALTH V. GOOD	
			WORK Repairs to Villages	
			Strength of Company at :- O R	
			beginning of month 5 . 79	
			Strength of End of month 3 . 59	

30-4-19

WAR DIARY
INTELLIGENCE SUMMARY

83rd FIELD COY R.E.

MAY 1919

Army Form C. 2118.

Place	Date	Hour	Summary of Events and Information	Remarks and references to Appendices
FAMECHON (5F 65 72)	May 1919 1st to 31st		Calm & company awaiting orders for demobilisation. Capt R.M.F. HUDDART demobilized on U.K. 13/5/19. Health very good. Strength of Coy at beginning of month 3 59 at end 2 26	

R.M. Huddart Capt
31-5-19

www.ingramcontent.com/pod-product-compliance
Lightning Source LLC
Chambersburg PA
CBHW081530160426
43191CB00011B/1731